FAMOUS FRETS

Steve Clarke

FAMOUS FRETS

Steve Clarke

WP
WYMER
PUBLISHING
Bedford, England

First published in Great Britain in 2019
by Wymer Publishing
www.wymerpublishing.co.uk
Tel: 01234 326691
Wymer Publishing is a trading name of Wymer (UK) Ltd

978-1-912782-25-3 Hardback
978-1-912782-22-2 Paperback

Book design by Steve Clarke and Danny Lee
Front cover design by Steve Clarke
Printed and bound in England by Halstan & Co. Ltd.

A catalogue record for this book is available from the British Library.

CONTENTS

Introduction

How did it come to this? Well, throughout many years of writing music, recording, touring and producing music I was always surprised at just how many guitarists would pay a lot of money for their instruments yet never know how to maintain them or even keep them in tune. Frequently, I would leave my seat in the control room to find that the strings had been on so long for gigs and rehearsals by the time they got in the studio the strings had lost their zing. I've seen Gibson and Fender guitars in such poor states of repair that you'd think they were a budget first guitar!

I always had a fascination for how some of the great guitars sounded the way they do. What combination of woods, electronics and set up combined to give such an individual voice? I wanted to know what was special about the combination of guitar model, string gauges, amp settings, pick-ups that made my heroes achieve their unique sound.

Some years ago I was coming back from holiday and whilst waiting at a train station I bought a guitar magazine. It struck me that although there was an abundance of articles dedicated to new models I was left bored and wanting something else. I couldn't find much in magazines or forums about iconic guitars other than a lot of speculation and urban myths. I decided there and then to phone the editor of Guitar and Bass magazine (now The Guitar Magazine) to ask why iconic models were not featured very often. I said surely I wasn't the only guitarist that would like to know about some of the guitars that had produced some of the most famous songs on the planet. The editor agreed and said quickly "you can't get close enough to them and in any case we'd never get permission to pull them apart". I said "well I take guitars apart every day for a living, what if I can get to them and do it, would you be interested in the articles?" "Yes, he said, good luck with that".

So, I then had to find my first challenge. As luck had it, I was now home fixing a guitar listening to the radio one evening. An introduction came on the radio stating that the next programme was called the Kalamazoo Girls and the presenter was Suzi Quatro. I listened intently to her enthusiasm speaking to the ladies at the Gibson factory about what it was like working at one of the biggest guitar companies around. Suzi also mentioned that she personally went to the Kalamazoo factory to buy her Les Paul bass guitar before coming to the UK. Suzi had huge success in the UK and I remember her playing that bass on the UK TV show Top of the Pops for her hit single 'Can the Can'. "That's it," I thought, where is that bass today, does she still have it? Next day I set to the task of tracking her down. After several phone calls I had a contact to enable me to ask her that very question. I find out that she still had the bass and better still, I can go to her house to review it. After a short email exchange I find out she is also willing to let me take it apart to look inside. During my visit I was able to tell her more about her bass: things she didn't know. I also did some maintenance on it while I was there.

The editor was true to his word and the article was published in the magazine in March 2015 and that kick started a passion to do more. As you will see in this book I have been incredibly fortunate to look at many historical guitars, some of them in great detail too. I hope you will find the content interesting. It hasn't been easy in some cases to get all of the information I'd have liked as time was sometimes against me. In this book I bring you information and measurements giving details never published before, photographs never seen before. I am hugely grateful to the artists/owners themselves for trusting me with these precious instruments and to the contacts who have helped me connect with these guitars, some that I thought had been lost forever. Such as the Paul Kossoff Stripped Burst used on the classic single 'All Right Now' or the Prince Cloud guitar or Jimi Hendrix's acoustic. I hope I have brought you closer to knowing just a little bit more about what makes these guitars sound so special in the hands of the world's greatest players.

Steve Clarke

Angus Young of AC/DC - Gibson L6-S 1973

AC/DC are an Australian band formed in 1973 by brothers Malcolm and Angus Young. Their albums have sold in colossal numbers estimated to be around 100 million worldwide. They are considered by many to be the pioneers of hard rock and Angus Young can play killer riffs that would have you head banging within ten seconds. Although later he would be associated with the Gibson SG, the early years show Angus using this guitar. This Gibson L6-S belonged to Malcolm and Angus Young. It is a 1973 model that Malcolm had professionally converted to a double cutaway. Angus then used it in the mid 70's evidenced in pictures from AC/DC's gig at the London Marquee Club where they had a residency. Malcolm later removed the front pickup and surround which were lost. According to original bassist Mark Evans, Mal bought the guitar from Harry Landis of Park Street, Sydney in early 1975. The L6-S was purchased because his Gretsch Jet Firebird had one of its many headstock breaks and was in the repair shop. Mal needed a guitar so he bought the Gibson. It was this guitar he was using until the Gretsch was fixed when Evans joined the band in March 1975: it then became a spare and was rarely used. The guitar was customised to the double cut in May/June 1976 in London by Martin Birch in Kentish Town. Evans went with Mal Young to drop it off. Once repaired, the guitar was then used all throughout the 'Bon Scott years' and was last seen on the Back in Black tour of 1980 when Stevie Young (nephew of Malcolm and Angus) used the guitar when playing support to AC/DC.

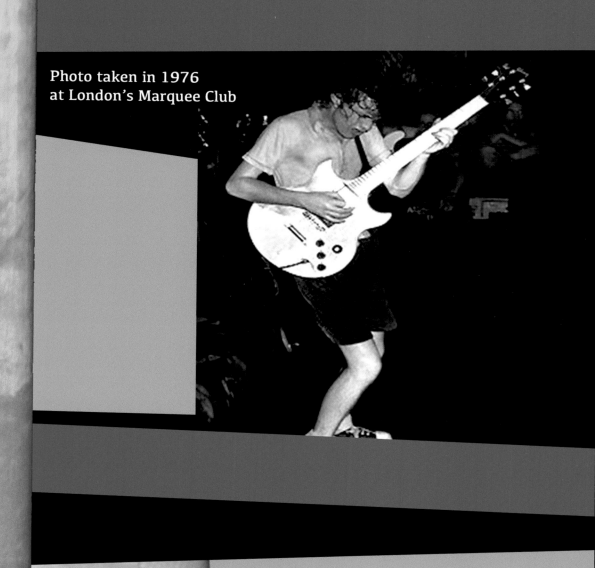

Photo taken in 1976
at London's Marquee Club

First impressions show the body is in good condition with no noticeable damage and the lacquer finish appears good too. The weight is 7.60lbs and the body thickness is 33mm/1⁵⁄₁₆″ on the upper horn and 33.64mm/1⁵⁄₁₆″ on the lower.

Around 12,000 L6-S Custom guitars were built typically with a three piece neck made of maple with maple, rosewood or ebony finger boards and a three piece maple body. The controls were a six position pickup selector, master volume, mid range, and a treble roll off control. When it was introduced, the L6-S Custom was simply called the L6-S: the Custom badge came later when the L6-S Deluxe was introduced.

The nut measures 40.67mm/1¹⁰⁄₁₆", is made of bone and is highly polished. The nut slots on the G B and E strings are a little too deep and the wound strings are notched a little wide at the top but they are seated well and don't move. The clearance over the first fret is about right. Original Gibson spec is given as length 100.5cm/39½" and scale length is 62.8 cm/24¾" with a body length of 41.8cm/16½", 24 frets.

At 86.2mm/3⅜" in length and 14.27mm/⁹⁄₁₆" width, the bridge looks to be of Japanese origin, something you may expect to see on a 70's Ibanez guitar. It works fine but it is not original to this guitar: the original would have been a Schaller. The saddles are worn down and have the appearance of graphite. The bottom E saddle the most worn and all the strings are sitting just a bit lower in the slots than they should be. Adjustment is by two slotted screws that go into metal posts that are fixed into the body of the guitar. The tailpiece is made of aluminium which many guitarists claim improves the tone, but that depends on your perspective. It is worth trying a metal cast one though if you have this kind of tailpiece and listen to the difference. The other thing I observe about the bridge to tailpiece distance is that the strings are longer than say a Les Paul would be. I'm sure the extra distance from these two points would result in more harmonics.

The guitar only has one pickup. It was designed by Bill Lawrence for Gibson and measures 6.20 ohms. Although not high output, the sound of this non adjustable pickup is very pleasing. Bill Lawrence made similar pickups for Framus in the same year this guitar was built. Taking the pickup out reveals a black epoxy resin covering the underneath. There are two wires coming out of the main grey wire which have a clear epoxy at the ends of them and a red ground wire soldered to the pickup adjustment heel.

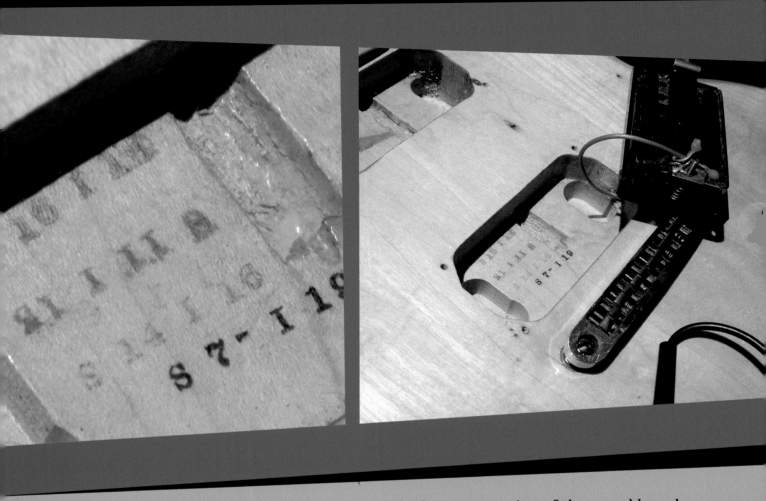

Never judge a book by its cover. In this case I had an expectation of the sound based upon the pictures I'd seen. Wrong! Plugging into a Marshall 100 watt Plexi and a 4x12 cab I am rewarded with a more versatile sound than many conventional guitars equipped with two

humbuckers. The 6-way rotary selector switch is missing the chicken head pointer knob revealing a broken split shaft but it is still operational giving three distinctive sounds and when used with the two tone controls, you get a really individual voice. One setting increases an edge and gain with different mid range voicing's, this is where the two tone controls work brilliantly together.

The original design of the L6-S wiring is ingenious. The aim was to give the guitar a wide variety of tone that would appeal to rock players. Carlos Santana was one of the first players to use it to great effect. The guitar had a Varitone circuit, two super humbuckers to allow the pickups to be used singly or together, in phase or out of phase, wired in series or in parallel. The tonal combinations are huge. Interestingly, this six position tone switch can also be found on the Framus Jan Akkerman guitar produced in 1974 and offered very similar sounds.

There is no mistaking the one sound in particular that takes you instantly into AC/DC territory. When I plug in the Gibson L6-S there is an unmistakable character of Angus. I'm sure the maple build of this guitar and front pickup cavity add to the resonance. In comparison to several Les Pauls ranging from the mid 50's P90 equipped Les Paul to a 1969 Les Paul Custom with humbuckers it was fascinating to note the subtle differences between them all.

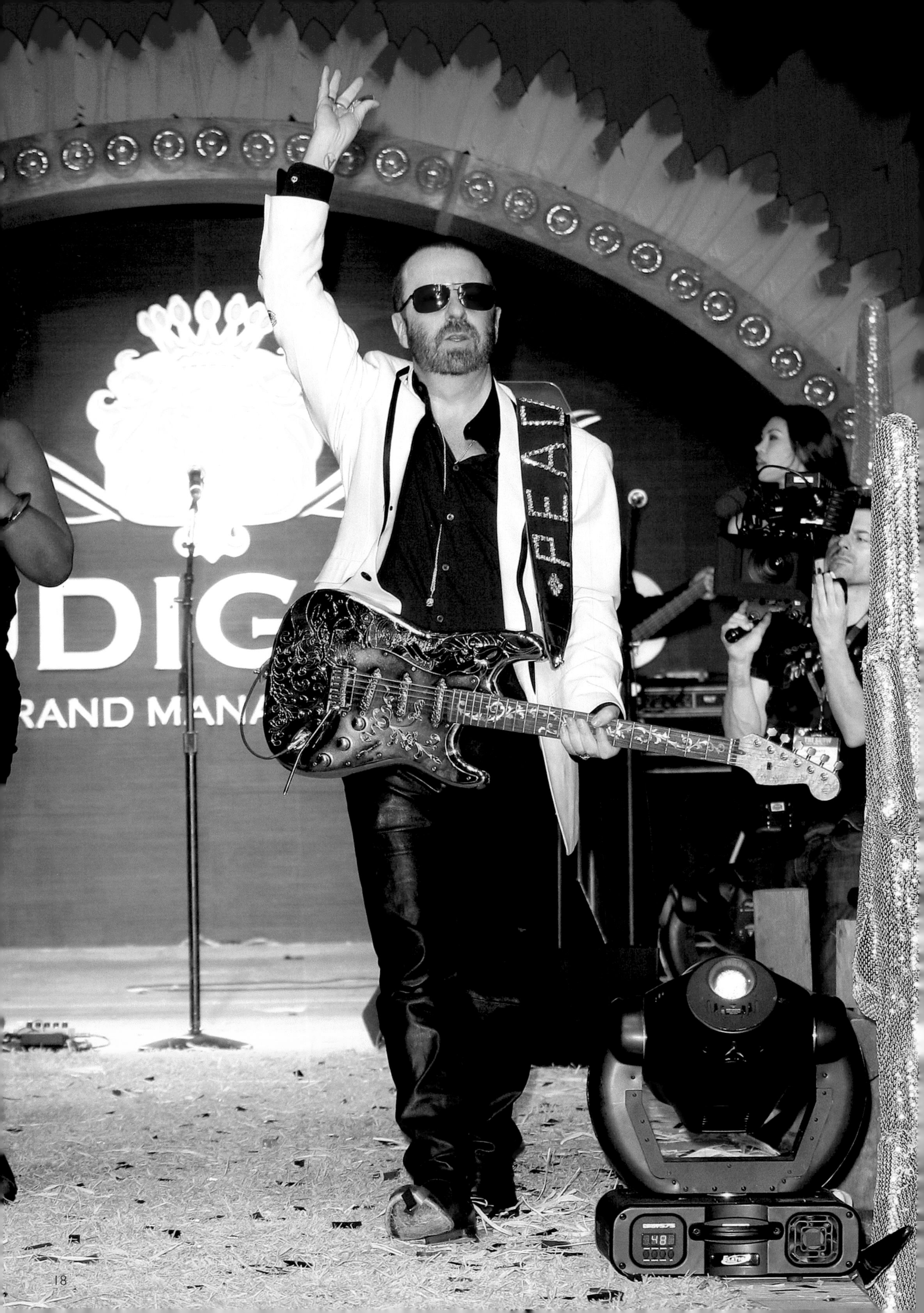

UDIG
RAND MANA
PEA

Dave Stewart 1993 Custom Shop Aluminium Strat

I recieved a phone call before the premier of Ghost The Musical at The Royal Exhange, Manchester to be the guitar tech for Dave Stewart at this event. Whilst speaking to Dave at the venue he told me that the guitars had just come up from Abbey Road Studios where he'd been working for the past couple of weeks. The Duesenberg guitar needed the most TLC as the strings had only just been put on slack and not tuned up. This is not a good thing with a Bigsby type guitar as the Bigsby demands more pre-stretching of the strings and thus they need playing in really well to achieve and hold the correct tuning. He told me the aluminium strat is one of only two known to be made by Fender Custom shop: Bob Dylan has the other one. The thing I noticed about this guitar was its great sustain, thick and full bodied sound. It was probably naive of me but because of it's aluminium construction I presumed it may sound thin and tinny. The weight was that of an average strat. The bottom E string was noticeably lower on the bridge than the other strings, this can cause intonation problems. I asked Dave about this and he said although unusual, he preferred the feel of it that way. To compensate, the treble side was slightly higher giving better tuning. When I plugged the guitar in I checked the pickups. The bridge pickup has great output with a really nice ring to it: not overly harsh or cutting. The middle pickup was as you'd expect with a good honky sound but when used in the out of phase setting with the bridge pickup it had an instant funk sound: think Play That Funky Music on steroids!

The middle pickup and neck combo is great for rhythm: not too bassy and would work great with a chorus pedal. The neck pickup on its own has wonderful articulation, each note delivers a nice harmonic ring and sustain. Considering there are no visble pole pieces, (it's just got engraved pickup cans on the top) the balance was wonderful.

These images were taken at The Royal Exchange, Manchester 2010

This is called the Duesenberg Starplayer MC, Tom Petty and the Heartbreakers 30th Anniversary Edition. It was given to Dave Stewart by Mike Campbell from the Heartbreakers. Dave Stewart used it on his album 'The Blackbird Diaries' and also on Joss Stones' album LP1.

The Brian Calhoun built 'Rock Fabulous' acoustic had a really well fitted nut, nicely cut and low, the neck was thin and fast and the action was low. The frets were impeccable as you'd expect and all this needed was new strings well stretched and it was good to go. Dave was concerned about the acoustic sounds in the theatre so I had to spend some time EQ-ing the guitar through the theatre desk to reduce reflective sound problems caused by the fact that the Royal Exchange Theatre is designed in the round so there is a lot of sound boom, bounce and reflection (natural echo).

Below:
Dave Stewart at the premier of the musical 'GHOST', at Manchester UK Royal Exchange Theatre, with Glen Ballard on keys.

I am travelling to the North East of England for what is perhaps the last chance to get a close look at a guitar that belonged to the late Paul Kossoff of Free. The owner, has very kindly allowed me to have a look in detail at the guitar. Gibson did a tribute in 2012 and I reviewed the VOS model in the August 2012 Volume 3 – no.11 Guitar and Bass Magazine. One hundred aged replica guitars were made with great attention to detail and two hundred and fifty VOS versions. I am today going to look at the original guitar. I was in a covers band in the late 70's and the North East was like a second home to me: we must have played every club and pub that existed three times over. Like many musicians one of my memories was the thrill of playing songs by Free: in my case, "All Right Now" or "Wishing Well". To say Paul Kossoff was an inspiration and influence on me is truly an understatement. As well as his incredible vibrato of which Eric Clapton once asked "how do you do that" he also played the most full chords, rarely playing standard D, E or G shapes. I sit down and over a cup of tea I asked Arthur Ramm, the current owner, how he came to own the guitar. He told me his band Beckett was supporting Free in 1972 at the Mayfair in Newcastle: it was the last night before Free was to split. Kossoff threw the guitar into the air breaking the neck and walked off the stage into the dressing room. In the dressing room Kossoff spotted Arthur's 68' refinished Gold Top Les Paul. Arthur was out of the room so Kossoff's roadie went to look for him. Arthur went into the dressing room to find Kossoff with the gold top round his neck. Kossoff asked him if he could borrow his guitar for a couple of songs saying he'd be very careful with it. When he came off stage Kossoff told Arthur his guitar was lovely and asked if he wanted to swap. Arthur said "well, you've broken yours!" to which Kossoff said "well, I've got this other one" and pointed to a case containing the stripped finish burst Les Paul used at the Isle of Wight in 1970. He told Kossoff that if he got the broken one fixed he'd prefer that one. So Arthur actually had the Isle of Wight guitar for many months whilst waiting for the other one to be repaired. Then one night, at Hamburg in the Top Ten Club his roadie put the guitar in the case and had only closed one latch on it. They were walking out of the club and down an alleyway when suddenly the guitar case opened and the guitar fell out onto a cobbled street. Arthur looked at his roadie and said "what's one more dent". Anyway, by the time the sunburst Les Paul was fixed, Kossoff had decided that he wanted to keep it. Arthur travelled to London to see Paul when he was living at Golborne Mews off the Portobello Road in order to return the stripped finished Les Paul in exchange for his own. They kept in touch and met up whenever Kossoff was in the North East. This sunburst Les Paul was even used by Phil Manzanera of Roxy Music on the OGWT on the track. In Every House a Heartache. This happened because Kossoff swapped the sunburst Les Paul for a three-pickup Black Custom belonging to John Porter, the bass player in Roxy Music, who then lent the sunburst guitar to Manzanera. Kossoff then got the guitar back again, and used it in his new band Back Street Crawler up to his death in 1976.

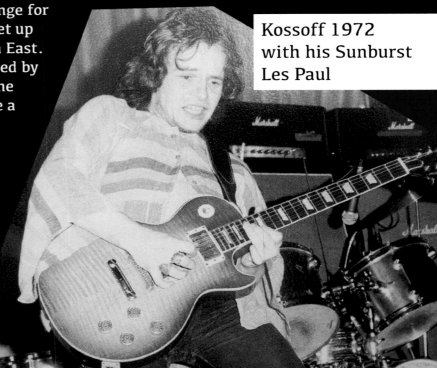

Kossoff 1972 with his Sunburst Les Paul

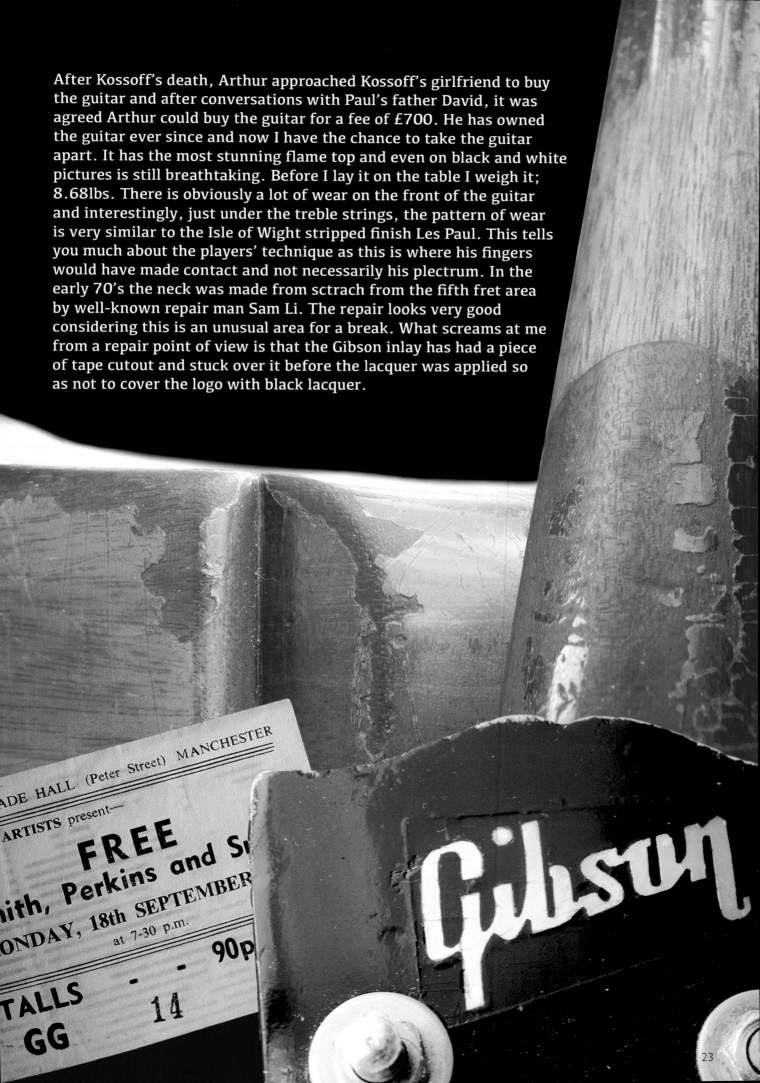

After Kossoff's death, Arthur approached Kossoff's girlfriend to buy the guitar and after conversations with Paul's father David, it was agreed Arthur could buy the guitar for a fee of £700. He has owned the guitar ever since and now I have the chance to take the guitar apart. It has the most stunning flame top and even on black and white pictures is still breathtaking. Before I lay it on the table I weigh it; 8.68lbs. There is obviously a lot of wear on the front of the guitar and interestingly, just under the treble strings, the pattern of wear is very similar to the Isle of Wight stripped finish Les Paul. This tells you much about the players' technique as this is where his fingers would have made contact and not necessarily his plectrum. In the early 70's the neck was made from sctrach from the fifth fret area by well-known repair man Sam Li. The repair looks very good considering this is an unusual area for a break. What screams at me from a repair point of view is that the Gibson inlay has had a piece of tape cutout and stuck over it before the lacquer was applied so as not to cover the logo with black lacquer.

ADE HALL (Peter Street) MANCHESTER

ARTISTS present—

FREE

ith, Perkins and Si

ONDAY, 18th SEPTEMBER

at 7-30 p.m.

90p

TALLS - - -

GG 14

The heel is typical of a 59' although I've read that because it's lost is serial number it could be a 58', 59' or 60' there are some clues to help narrow the date down. Firstly, 58' Les Pauls don't usually have such flame tops and can be quite plain. The necks are bigger in the hand and the heel larger too, but as always, exceptions do exist. 59' Les Pauls started to have slightly more rounded and slimmer necks with smaller heels and more appeared with flame tops with a variety of striking effects. Looking at a colour picture of Paul Rogers playing this guitar backstage in 1972 you can see the beautiful sunburst finish this guitar originally had with plenty of red visible. The nut width is 43mm/1¹¹⁄₁₆″ and at the 16th fret I take a measurement of 55mm/2³⁄₁₆″. The original nylon nut that was on the guitar is now broken near the A and E strings (although not completely split) is still in the guitar case.

The bridge is not an original tune-o-matic ABR1 as this one has the retaining wire that stops the saddles falling out, although the bottom E saddle is more worn and the screw head is not bevelled like the other screw heads are. Originally they would have been nickel plated brass. The bridge has been on the guitar since Arthur bought it so Kossoff played it with this bridge fitted.

I'm pretty sure this guitar is an early 59',probably in the 9-280's to 9-300's, although the serial number is lost.I've seen a 59' in this number range and although not accurate in a chronological sense, it can give batch information on the output Gibson used.I've also seen this number range on another Les Paul that could have come off the same billet as the Kossoff guitar that too had black coil Humbuckers. The neck pickup is

Andy Fraser, the last person in 'Free' to play this guitar

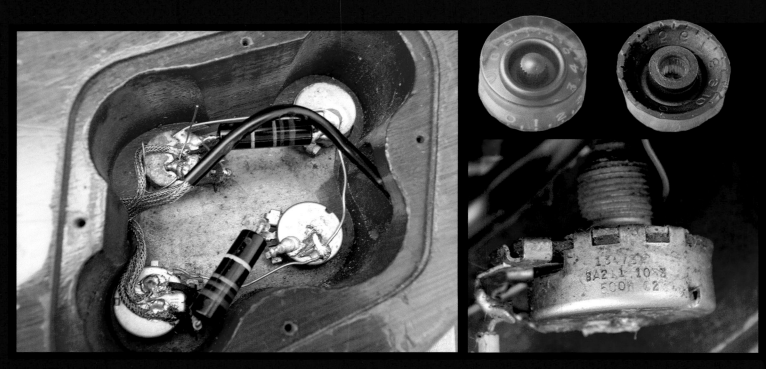

The bridge pickup has a lot of attack and is not too bright but is edgy going through a clean channel on a small Fender Combo. Quick chord changes with open strings give such shimmer to the notes with not one string being dominant, on overdrive, this is one hell of a loud pickup! The middle position does not overwhelm as is often the case with some modern Humbuckers but it gives a full mid range sound with just enough bass. The neck pickup is creamy and full of depth: a wonderful wailing blues tone. This is such a comfortable neck with frets leaning more to the jumbo type: it makes bending notes a breeze.

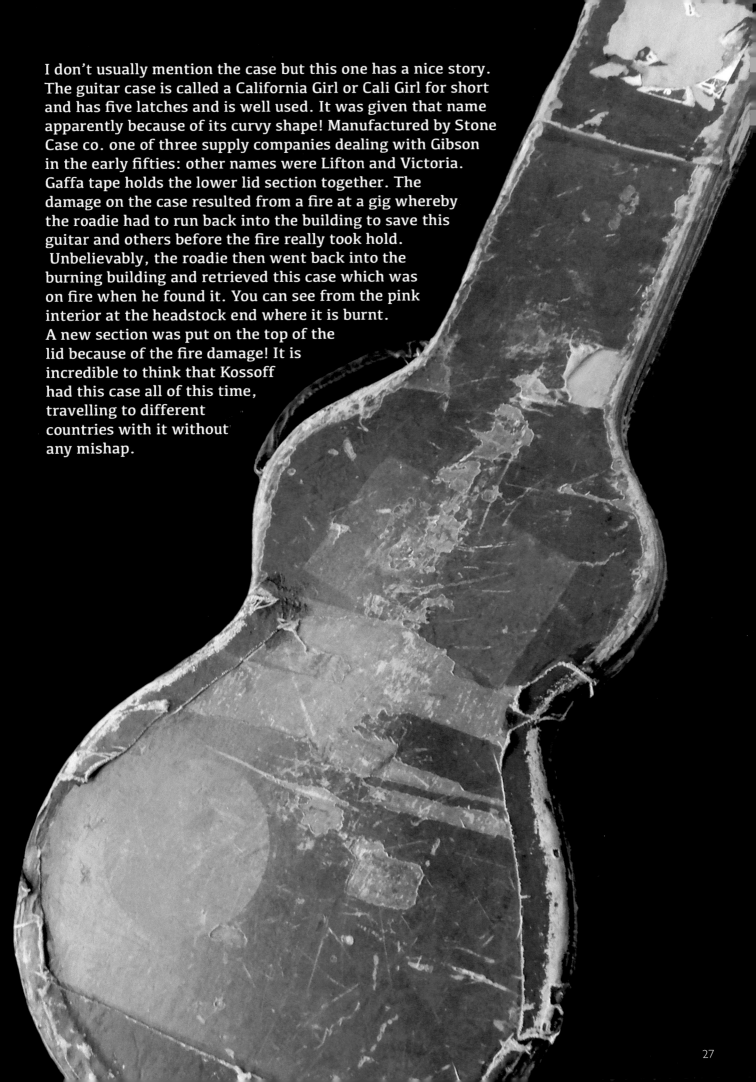

I don't usually mention the case but this one has a nice story. The guitar case is called a California Girl or Cali Girl for short and has five latches and is well used. It was given that name apparently because of its curvy shape! Manufactured by Stone Case co. one of three supply companies dealing with Gibson in the early fifties: other names were Lifton and Victoria. Gaffa tape holds the lower lid section together. The damage on the case resulted from a fire at a gig whereby the roadie had to run back into the building to save this guitar and others before the fire really took hold. Unbelievably, the roadie then went back into the burning building and retrieved this case which was on fire when he found it. You can see from the pink interior at the headstock end where it is burnt. A new section was put on the top of the lid because of the fire damage! It is incredible to think that Kossoff had this case all of this time, travelling to different countries with it without any mishap.

FREE TRADE HALL, Peter Street, Manchester

VIRGIN CONCERTS present

**The
Paul Kossoff Band**
Plus SUPPORT

Saturday, 17th May, 1975
at 7.30 p.m.

No money refunds or ticket exchanges. Official Brochures
sold ONLY in the Theatre.

Friedlander Press 061-792 4929

STALLS

DD 3 4 75P.
inc. vat

It would be pure speculation to suggest what songs this guitar has been played on but the album Free At Last and Free Live is very likely. The fact Kossoff had this guitar up until 1976 is testament that he liked this one. Kossoff swapped his black three-pickup Les Paul Custom for Eric Clapton's' 1958 Darkburst Les Paul on the 1969 Blind Faith tour, and it has been said that he used the Darkburst to record All Right Now. The song was recorded at Trident studios on the 11th January 1970 and released in May, but on Top of the Pops, Kossoff is using the stripped finish Les Paul which he bought in Spring 1969 before the recording. You will see later the story on the Stripped Burst about this

Paul Kossoff has been an inspiration to many established guitarists, and he continues to find a place in the technical aspirations of guitarists who soon realise the construction of a solo is often more about the notes you leave out. Kossoff had a remarkable ability to play several notes between Paul Rogers' vocals without going too far, and thus produced the most emotive playing with an intense vibrato that to this day makes him stand apart from the fast and furious. In the short time Kossoff was with us, he managed to create a lasting legacy and anyone wanting to express feeling, tone and expression through their playing, will have a hard time finding anyone who could do it better than Paul Kossoff!

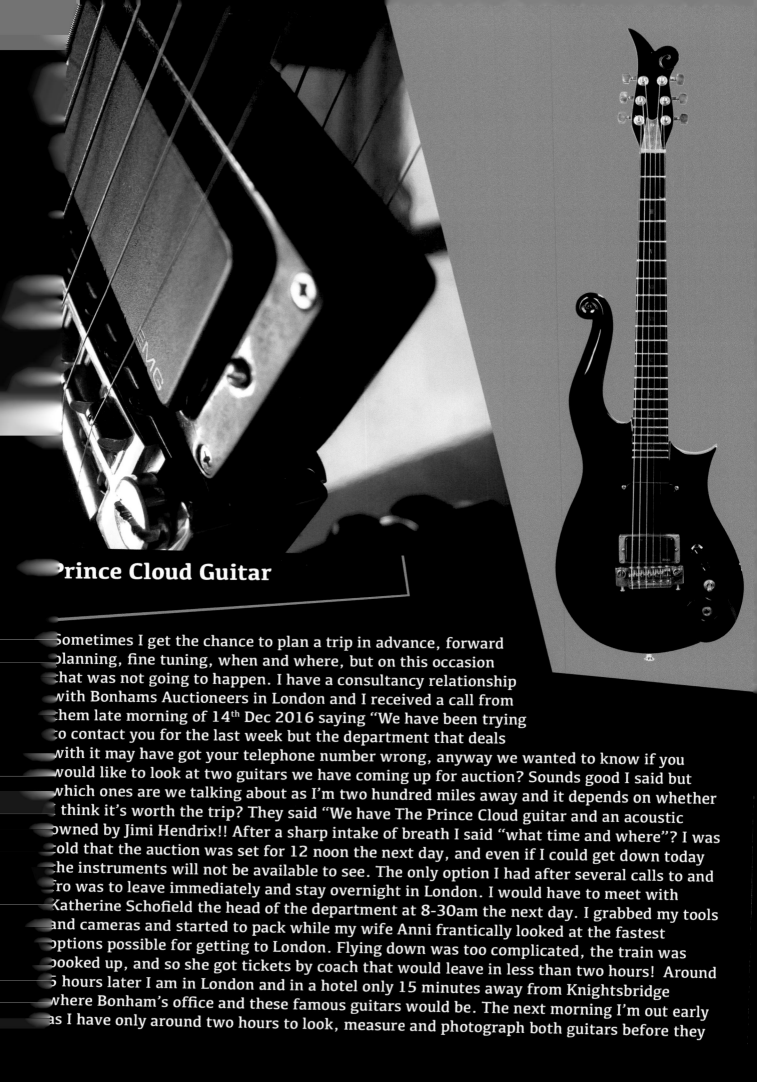

Prince Cloud Guitar

Sometimes I get the chance to plan a trip in advance, forward planning, fine tuning, when and where, but on this occasion that was not going to happen. I have a consultancy relationship with Bonhams Auctioneers in London and I received a call from them late morning of 14th Dec 2016 saying "We have been trying to contact you for the last week but the department that deals with it may have got your telephone number wrong, anyway we wanted to know if you would like to look at two guitars we have coming up for auction? Sounds good I said but which ones are we talking about as I'm two hundred miles away and it depends on whether I think it's worth the trip? They said "We have The Prince Cloud guitar and an acoustic owned by Jimi Hendrix!! After a sharp intake of breath I said "what time and where"? I was told that the auction was set for 12 noon the next day, and even if I could get down today the instruments will not be available to see. The only option I had after several calls to and fro was to leave immediately and stay overnight in London. I would have to meet with Katherine Schofield the head of the department at 8-30am the next day. I grabbed my tools and cameras and started to pack while my wife Anni frantically looked at the fastest options possible for getting to London. Flying down was too complicated, the train was booked up, and so she got tickets by coach that would leave in less than two hours! Around 5 hours later I am in London and in a hotel only 15 minutes away from Knightsbridge where Bonham's office and these famous guitars would be. The next morning I'm out early as I have only around two hours to look, measure and photograph both guitars before they

I arrive 8-30 sharp and could see in the distance Katherine approaching, we walk into this fabulous auction house. The guitars are already on display in the main auction room and we go straight to them. There on a guitar stand as I walk in was the Prince Cloud guitar, next to this was the Jimi Hendrix Epiphone FT79 built in 1951. I ask for a room with some natural light which was in short supply in December! I was escorted by security downstairs to a small room and asked if I could see the Prince guitar first. It was now past 9 o'clock and I am warned that both guitars have to be back on their stands by 11.15 as the media and TV people will be in the building wanting pictures, and to report live on the event.

I was given full permission to take apart the Prince guitar which was a wonderful trusting environment to be in. The background to this guitar is that it was used on the Act 1&2 Prince and the New Power Generation tour 1993. It has been kept by the vendor and has rarely been taken out of its case while in her possession since she won it in an MTV competition in 1993; the prize included travelling with the NPG band on their tour bus during the Act 2 tour in Germany, where she joined them in Munich and then on to Dusseldorf the following day. The whirlwind experience let her watch Prince on stage and even pick the clothes for him to wear that night! She met him afterwards and had a private performance by him. What was not part of the prize was this guitar, Prince just decided to give it to her! It was handed to her on stage by Levi Seacer JR, (NPG) guitarist at the Wildenrath Flugplatz in Wegberg before watching Prince perform. It also came with the original Paisley Park letter and touring itinerary and travelling paperwork

This guitar was built for Prince by Andy Beech in the USA. He also made the 'symbol' guitar that Prince used on Purple Rain during his half-time performance at the 2007 Super Bowl. Andy made a total of 31 guitars for Prince during the 1990s: 27 cloud guitars and 4 symbol guitars. After graduating from Mount Baker high school in 1983 Andy went to Hollywood. He met with Zakk Wylde who had just become guitarist for Ozzy Osborne's band and Andy became the guitar tech for Wylde on tour from 1991-1996. He also made guitars for Wylde including a guitar called The Glory. After time on the road, he decided to move back to Whatcom County where he started to do finishing work on expensive houses being built, but crafting guitars was where his heart was and it wasn't long before he opened D Haitre Guitars in Bellingham. I contacted Andy who very kindly sent me some Polaroid pictures of the cloud guitar being built.

Pictures courtesy of Andy Beech

Andy Beech

This guitar today is a thrill to see up close whilst getting some idea of its build and electrics. I take hold of the guitar and immediately I am aware of how light it is. It weighs 7.32 lbs which I am sure for Prince was something factored in for not only his smaller stature but to help with ease of dance moves in his performance. The frets measure 2.38mm/³⁄₃₂" and are impeccable on the black lacquered maple fingerboard. The second fret has had some touch up lacquer put on behind the fret wire. Taking a measurement at the 16th fret it's a slim 51.94mm/2¹⁄₃₂". The 22 fret fingerboard is decorated with Roman numerals and the scale is 628.65mm/24¾". At the headstock on a gold plated truss rod cover is a number 4 stamped into the metal as can be seen in photos of Prince with this guitar. The playing action is very low which came as no surprise.

I don't tune the guitar to pitch as the strings are old and worn looking: these would have been the strings that were on the guitar when Prince used it so I don't want to risk snapping any just before the sale. They appear to be 10s but like I say some corrosion is evident. After tuning the guitar a step down or so it feels really comfortable to play. Also surprising is the natural sustain the guitar has: this is probably due to the maple body and neck and the great coupling at the bridge end. The playability is excellent and no truss rod adjustment is needed. The nut measures 38.77mm/1½" and is made of brass, the bottom E string is high in the slot and the A string is similar. The D string is too deep but does not rattle on the first fret; GBE strings are all too deep in their slots, especially the G which is too wide. The clearance over the first fret overall is ok but you would expect more precision: having said that the D and G strings at the back of the nut do not have too much tension to pull them to the sides which would help tuning stability.

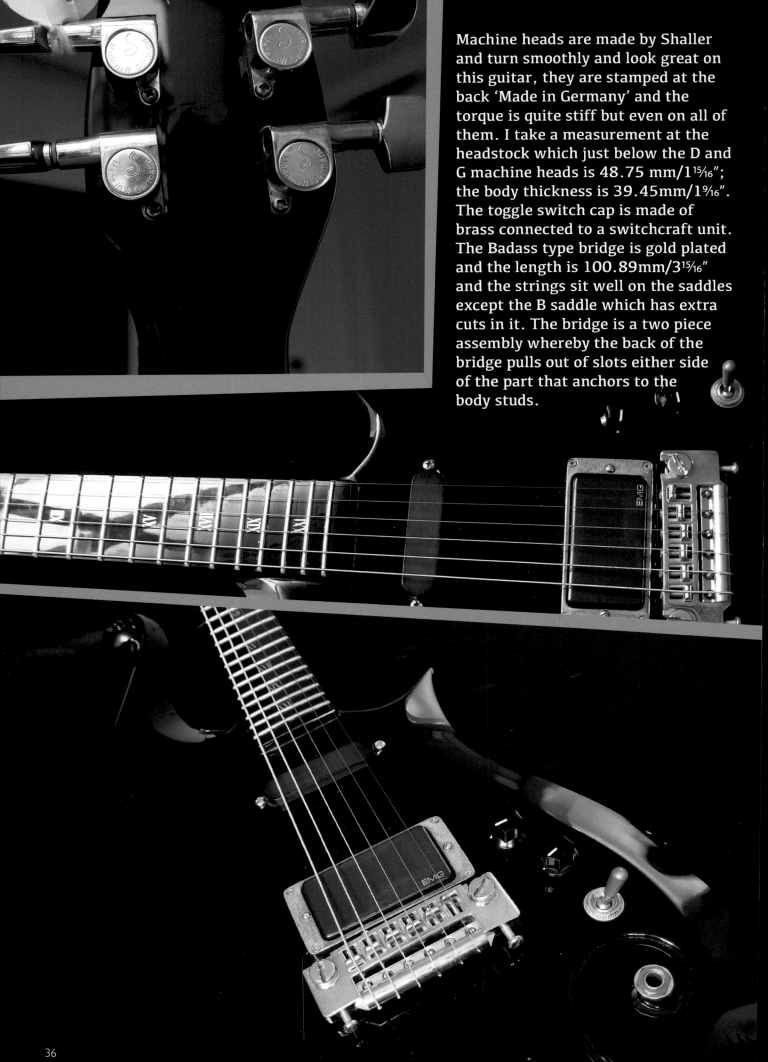

Machine heads are made by Shaller and turn smoothly and look great on this guitar, they are stamped at the back 'Made in Germany' and the torque is quite stiff but even on all of them. I take a measurement at the headstock which just below the D and G machine heads is 48.75 mm/1^{15}/$_{16}$"; the body thickness is 39.45mm/1^{9}/$_{16}$". The toggle switch cap is made of brass connected to a switchcraft unit. The Badass type bridge is gold plated and the length is 100.89mm/3^{15}/$_{16}$" and the strings sit well on the saddles except the B saddle which has extra cuts in it. The bridge is a two piece assembly whereby the back of the bridge pulls out of slots either side of the part that anchors to the body studs.

The pickups comprise an EMG-891JD humbucker in the bridge and a 5A single coil for the neck. I took a reading of the bridge pickup which is active but the battery is dead, none the less I got a flash reading of 17.51DC but a second attempt did not repeat this. The cavity shows some maple wood in places and the soldering is ok but surprisingly in parts not that good! Lacquer cracks can be seen at the back of the body and the strap button looks like it was moved from just behind the neck joint which measures 44.45mm/1¾". You can see where it's been filled in and lacquered over, the neck looks like a scarf joint lacquer crack but nothing serious.

Prince would often throw his guitar through the air to his tech: sometimes he would miss the catch and the neck would crack or even break. The balance of this guitar considering its unusual shape is very good; it's easy to see why Prince would feel comfortable with this guitar.

It's hard to believe that he is no longer with us, but his guitar playing stood out for its melodic solos and attack that few artists can achieve. Coupled with great song writing he was one of the most dynamic performers in the world.

 Paisley Park Enterprises

THE PRINCE GUITAR
"The Cloud Guitar"

We hereby confirm that the guitar presented to Sandra Pemberton at an MTV Europe competition by Levi Seacer of the NPG in August, 1993 as a contest prize is an authentic hand-built guitar as described below.

A guitar of unique beauty, the cloud begins as a neck through body design that gives it a very solid and sturdy construction with a one-piece look and feel.

Eastern hard rock maple is utilized throughout. This heavy wood is unsurpassed for its stable unforgiving strength, giving the small guitar a substantial feel without being too heavy. The hardware consists of precision schaller tuning gears and bridges, with an EMG 81 humbucher and 5A single coil pick ups.

All the hardware is triple gold plated machined brass, and polyester paints are used for its incredible durability and beautiful long lasting shine.

All these elements add up to make a very high quality custom guitar. The slim 1 1/2 and 24 3/4 scale make it easy to play.

Cloud guitars are custom made by Andy Beach in the USA for ⚤ (the artist formerly known as Prince).

Karen Lee, Vice President
Media Communications and Publicity

7801 Audubon Road, Chanhassen, MN 55317 • (612) 474-6630

Jimi Hendrix Epiphone 1951 FT79

Still at Bonhams, time was moving on so I asked for the Jimi Hendrix guitar to be brought into the room. This gave me just enough time to put the strings back on the Prince cloud guitar, bring them to tension, then it was taken away by the security staff. It's difficult to put into words sometimes just how lucky I have been looking at some of the most iconic guitars around, but just as I catch my breath, a guitar case comes into view from around the door held by security. This time it is believed to be the guitar Jimi Hendrix had in his possession almost three years, longer than any other guitar he owned, This guitar is a 1951 Epiphone FT 79: serial number 62262. Jimi can be seen with this guitar in a picture taken in London in1967. With money earned from the Monterey pop festival and some American shows, Jimi bought this second hand for about $25 in New York. It was brought back to England on the plane recalls Noel Redding. A picture taken on the tarmac at Heathrow Airport on August 21st 1967 shows this guitar being held by Noel Redding.

According to Kathy Etchingham his girlfriend at the time, this guitar became Jimi's favoured guitar at their Upper Berkeley Street flat. It was apparently used all the time. Manager Chas Chandler said that Jimi was so attached to his guitar that he would even take it to the bathroom with him. Having moved from a basement flat in Montague Square, London because of complaints about the noise, this Epiphone came into its own in their new flat that had a tiled bathroom with no window in it and thus had a wonderful echo that Jimi liked so much he would sit on the lavatory and play his guitar. Kathy states that he used the guitar for almost everything he composed in the UK as he didn't have an amp until he moved to Brook Street later on. When Jimi was working on a song he would pick up and play the acoustic, then pick up a Strat and play that without an amp. On this guitar he would work out the riffs in the song including arrangements notably on his version of Bob Dylan's "All Along the Watchtower ".

The guitar was used regularly following Jimi's move to Brook Street. This would be around the time Electric Ladyland was finished and can be seen in photographs taken at this time. There is also film of him playing the Elvis Presley song Hound Dog on this guitar at the after show party following The Experience's Royal Albert Hall concert on February 18th 1969. People who visited the Brook Street flat at this time remember the guitar was always within arm's reach, usually beside the bed.

In March 1970 Jimi gave the guitar to Alan Parker who was the guitarist with Blue Mink, having been introduced to him by Kathy's friend, Blue Mink's singer Madeleine Bell. The guitar was then use by Allan Parker on numerous recordings and sound tracks such as those by Dusty Springfield, The Walker Brothers, Blue Mink, Paul McCartney and David Bowie's Diamond Dogs. The guitar comes with a sheepskin guitar strap and non original hard case with the stencilled A. Parker on its lid.

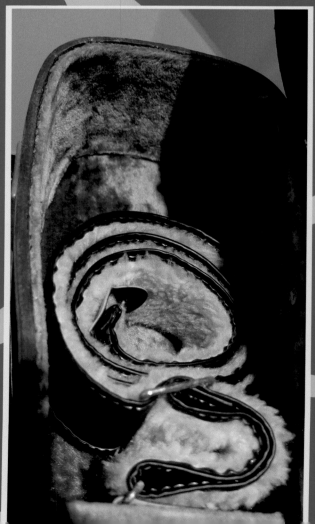

I place the guitar on a round table which wasn't ideal to work on as it was quite small, all the while just four feet away was a security guard watching my every move! I immediately notice that the binding in the middle waist on both sides is coming away, also the binding at the bottom of the guitar near the strap button is separating. Looking at the original pictures of Noel Redding holding the guitar on the tarmac at Heathrow Airport on August 21st 1967 there appears to be noticeable wear around the sound hole, a measurement taken here is 96.46mm/3^{13}⁄$_{16}$" across. Also the colour yellow sprayed from the middle of the guitar stops just outside the bridge area on both the treble and the bass sides of the solid spruce top. The tortoiseshell style scratchplate is lifting away from the top of the guitar likely because it was taken off and reapplied after the respray. Today the yellow is wider reducing the dark brown outer colour. There are many cracks and much checking in the finish. I think the top has had a re-spray many years ago which also resulted in the bridge having a light sanding and clear lacquer coat. The laminated maple back and sides and neck also appear to be resprayed, but it's still a beautiful colour.

The body thickness behind the bridge end is 101.93mm/4″ and it's clear that the bridge saddle has been changed at some point, saddle length is 88.67mm/3½″. Originally Epiphone would use an ebony saddle. Headstock thickness at the bottom E tuner is 17.70mm/^{11}⁄₁₆″, at the top above the D tuner it is 16.29mm/⅝″: this was how Gibson also tapered their necks but this Epiphone was made in the New York factory before Gibson acquired Epiphone. There has been a new nut fitted 42.29mm/1^{9}11⁄₁₆″. The headstock width at the top is 81.56mm/3¼″ and cracking covers most of this area. The frets are well cut and are 2.6mm/⅛″. The Brazilian rosewood fretboard is in very good condition with pearl inlays and a measurement at the 14th fret is 53.86 mm/2⅛″. The action is low and easy to play allowing for the fact I have to play the chords in a right handed way! It's also a comfortable 5.02 lbs. Hendrix was without a doubt the most influential guitarist of his time. Just about all the greats that came after 1970 up to modern times would site him as an influence and inspiration. It's impossible to imagine just how he may have developed his style if he had lived longer, except to say he was a already the most unique player you could ever witness, so maybe that's enough!

Marc Bolan 1959 Gibson Les Paul Standard (Road Warrior)

T.REX

Whenever we hear a record played on the radio it often evokes a memory that reminds us of a fashion trend and the music that inspired us. The power of music in its many forms could lift us up temporarily especially so when seeing that music played live. In the early 70s in the UK when strikes and power cuts were prevalent, the music scene needed a kick-start after the screaming had subsided from The Beatles and The Rolling Stones in their previous hit making decade.

It took one guy to do this: his name was Marc Bolan. After time as the underground outfit Tyrannosaurus Rex, consisting of Steve Peregrine Took on bongos and Marc Bolan on guitar. In April 1968 the song Deborah kick-started a success that was soon to explode into hysteria that hadn't been seen since Beatlemania. After a name change to simply T. REX and a switch of bongo player to Mickey Finn, in October 1970 the song Ride a White Swan was released and when Marc Bolan placed glitter under each eye and played the catchiest guitar riff to come out in years, the scene was set.

The song reached number two in the UK charts but by the time the second single Hot Love was released, a new, more confident Marc Bolan emerged helped by the fact the song stayed six weeks at number 1 in the UK chart! This was the start of what became known as Glam Rock. Colour TV was now appearing in homes and glam rock was made for it. Other groups copied: Slade, The Sweet, Wizzard, David Bowie, all soon adopted the colourful sparkly clothing and all of them had a string of hits. This was when selling a million copies of a single was common place.

The original neck in 1970 had Grover machine heads and the dot over the i on the Gibson logo, there was a gap between the nut and the truss rod cover as well as the scratch plate screw in the white binding. It moved lower on the second neck change during the Electric Warrior Tour on the 27th October 1971 gig. There is a picture that shows Bolan backstage at The Dome, Brighton, East Sussex, England. It still has the original neck! There could only be about a week to put a new neck on the guitar, because by the 6th November at the Manchester Free Trade Hall gig, England. The second neck has now appeared with the 21st fret missing and the i dot over the Gibson logo has gone!

tracks.co.uk

At the start of the Electric Warrior tour some film was shot and there is a very brief glimpse at the headstock that shows not only the Grovers still in place, but a serial number in a light colour on the back of the headstock. The only reasonable view to take is that whoever did the repair made note of the serial number before respraying the neck black, then put it back on for identification purposes. The neck stayed like this up to what was called in the media T.REXTASY. On March 18th 1972 Ringo Starr filmed two shows for the film Born to Boogie to capture what he described as hysteria not seen since Beatlemania. T. REX by now were the biggest selling group in the UK, the hits were coming thick and fast. Sometime in April 1972 is where the story of the neck takes another turn. On May 11th T.REX appeared on the BBC show Top of the Pops for their next number one hit Metal Guru, but now the neck is from a Les Paul custom with split diamond inlay and block markers with a blank truss rod cover with no i dot.

This neck is also black at the back, I don't believe as suggested that this was from his 1955 Les Paul custom as the truss rod cover is in the wrong place. Bolan did have in his collection though a two Humbucker equipped black custom bought around this time, could this of been the one cannibalised? I have never seen him with this particular guitar live and it may have been a spare. I spoke to George Gruhn (Gruhn's Guitars) and he said "I cannot see Gibson sending out a neck this quick and having it fitted in this short time". Now here comes the interesting bit, just after the TOTP's appearance 11th May 1972, T. REX were to start a mini tour of the UK starting at the Birmingham Odeon on 9th June, but on the next Top of the Pops performance 24th May, Bolan was using a metal fronted Zamaitis guitar. Could this be because this was whilst the Les Paul was being fitted with yet another neck!

When T. REX played the mini tour, the Les Paul custom neck had gone! It is now featuring what looks like a copy custom neck with the first fret block marker missing and all the inlays are smaller. The split diamond headstock associated with the custom has gone and is more like a standard. Pictures show that the back of the neck is now natural wood. The machine heads look like Grovers again possibly taken from previous necks, also the Gibson logo has the i dot back again This neck looks like it was totally made from scratch. Was this the known repairman Sam Li at work? On 16th June gig at Belle Vue Manchester England, (the gig Morrissey from UK band The Smiths attended) the neck broke again. I was at this show and Bolan had trouble tuning his guitar and changed it to a Gibson Flying V and Bolan referenced this in the pop paper NME a week later. It was not a complete neck break and may have just been a crack that had movement but was glued, because the same neck is still in place 24th June at Newcastle City Hall: the last gig. However, by the time the track Children of the Revolution was released, T.REX then appeared on TOTP's 14th September which reveals another Gibson Les Paul custom neck has been fitted with split diamond headstock. The machine heads though are now Schaller types and are bevelled at the side of the buttons. The guitar stays this way up to the beginning of January 1977 when it went missing.

To the right the guitar as it looks today, below is a mock up of how it looked in 1970

Some years later around 1994 the guitar appeared in an advertisement selling a Les Paul Standard in sunburst, but it had been resprayed all black previously, nobody knew anything about its history until it was stripped back to the finish under the black lacquer. It was then that certain details started to appear that could be seen in the grain pattern that identified it as the missing Bolan guitar. The neck has changed once more and is now more like the original standard neck with the crown inlays that we saw on this guitar in 1970. This makes a total number of six necks this guitar has had including its original one!

ORIGINAL NECK

NECK TWO
(21st FRET MISSING)

NECK THREE
(LES PAUL CUSTOM NECK)

NECK FOUR
(COPY CUSTOM NECK)

NECK FIVE
(LES PAUL CUSTOM NECK)
BACK AGAIN

The harmonics are rich and the balance of sound is not dominant in the bass which is nice. The mid position sounds almost out of phase; this could be due to the neck pickup being higher in DC. It is by no means thin and weedy and is a great rhythm setting for chord work or arpeggios.

The neck pickup is a zebra PAF; it measures 8.36 ohms and is in a class of its own. You are greeted with wonderfully rich tones and balance across the strings. The tone control takes out the top treble frequencies

> **That guitar was used on Get It On, Jeepster, Motivator; on most the tracks on Electric Warrior.**
>
> - Tony Visconti

but retains a beautiful midrange articulation. This is probably one of the nicest front PAFs I have heard and the pole pieces don't seem to have been adjusted much over the years, as when you turn any one of them around, the metal is quite clean compared to the very dark colour on the top. Sometimes you can see Bolan using this pickup on a live solo and there is evidence of its presence on the classic album Electric Warrior. I contacted Tony Visconti to ask if he had any memory of what tracks this guitar would have been used on, this is what he had to say.... "Anytime you heard a Les Paul from Marc it was that one. He didn't have a second one when I was working with him. That guitar was used on Get It On, Jeepster, Motivator; on most the tracks on Electric Warrior. When he wasn't using the LP he was using the white Strat with the teardrop decal glued to it. My girlfriend Liz Hartley made that for him. I think Marc also played the LP on The Wizard (but not sure) and Diamond Meadows. He was an amazing, unique player."

The neck at first looks ok from several feet away, but on closer inspection things change dramatically. The thickness at the low E side tuner is 16.34mm/⅝", which tapers to the D string giving 14.67mm/⁹⁄₁₆", (the Paul Kossoff isle of white Les Paul measures 16.26mm/⅝" and 14.55mm/⁹⁄₁₆" which is remarkably close but this neck is not all what it seems). The cut is wrong on the pearloid inlays and the 21st fret has a huge gap around it. The binding has these strange bumps all the way along the fingerboard on both sides because when it was refretted, the fret tang was not filed and sanded to the rosewood edge, when the binding was glued and clamped, the resulting feel is lumpy!

 The jumbo frets measure 3.21mm/⅛" and are not a great idea for intonation. Gibson experimented with large wire in the 70s but many guitarists complained of similar problems and had them changed due to the string length, as going further up the neck with thick wire changed accuracy. There is a whole science to this and manufacturers are well aware of the tolerances. The headstock face has something going on under the lacquer in front of the truss rod cover, it looks like some damage has happened and filled in badly and sprayed over. The Gibson logo looks ok though but my feeling is that this neck was made up of parts. The rosewood fingerboard has been put onto a mahogany neck and the inlays put in roughly with not much care. This neck has reportedly been made by a luthier and some of the measurements do come close to what it should be, but in my opinion there's no care in the final result. The headstock width at the top is 78.74mm/3⅛", (the Kossoff is 78.54mm) and with what looks like a holly or maple veneer on the headstock face, I'm impressed with the measurements. The machine heads are Grover and work perfectly, although a little stiff. It has had another set before these, probably Kluson as the holes top and bottom testifies. The nut is 42.42mm/1¹⁰⁄₁₆", again for comparison the Kossoff nut is 42.56mm. This one is made of Nylon as the original standards were. By the way the name Nylon was a collaboration of the two cities involved in its development, New York and London!

The nut does not fit to the edges of the neck and the nut slots are too deep for the strings which are another problem area. The first fret distance to the underside string is too low to hit an E chord without some rattle. The ABR-1 nickel plated bridge has had new saddles and unfortunately has dipped in the middle, it looks to be original though and is wearing in the right places and some plating is coming off. It really needs straightening out in a clamp to put this back. The saddles could do with some cutting as the wound strings sit on top too much. The bridge posts are loose and make the bridge tilt forward a little, some glue has been put in the holes but it is the wrong thing to do. The bridge measures 83.53mm/3⅜", width 10.66mm/⁷⁄₁₆", and post to post centre top thread is 72.23mm/2¹³⁄₁₆".

The tailpiece looks to be the original aluminium unit at 101.46mm/3¹⁵⁄₁₆" length and 17.49mm/¹¹⁄₁₆" width. You can see from photographs of Bolan playing this guitar that it was once actually gold plated, evidence of this is just visible underneath the tailpiece where there are some gold flakes left. This also looks like the original tailpiece as well as the studs which secure it. It is interesting to note that when Gibson did the Marc Bolan tribute guitar, they forgot the toggle switch was not plastic but a metal one taken off a Gretsch guitar.

The metal studs are 12.08mm/½″ wide bass side and 12.72mm/½″ wide treble side. The toggle is an original switchcraft and still works fine, the poker chip surround measures 33.84mm/1⁵⁄₁₆″ and the nut securing the toggle is 15.77mm/⅝″, both are original. The bonnet style, or hat knobs look also to be original but one of them is broken but has been glued. Looking underneath there is the typical green tinge you get on these old knobs. Looking at the edges of the volume control it also has a slight worn look to it unlike the tone controls which are slightly sharper.

The metal pointers are original and a bit rusty but nice to see they have survived. The control knob lower skirt measures 25.98mm/1¹⁄₃₂″ and the upper part is 17.49mm/¹¹⁄₁₆″. The body on this guitar has obviously been sanded down at least three times and measures' 45.55mm/1¹³⁄₁₆″ at the lower cutaway: at the tailpiece end it is 45.17mm/1¹³⁄₁₆″. The inside lower cutaway near the maple cap is 53.54mm/2⅛″, and just above the toggle switch it is 46.48mm/1¹³⁄₁₆″. The maple cap toward the middle of the guitar would be approx 13mm/½″ maple, and the thinnest part is around 3mm/⁴⁄₃₂″. Original 59 Les Pauls would average at the tailpiece end around just over 48mm/1¹⁴⁄₁₆″. Due to sanding it's reasonable to expect this discrepancy. The body still has a lot of battle scars and has been played over the years and not put away. The maple cap is the clue to this guitars history from the pictures I have seen. Even allowing for colour changes and sanding, the grain is still there.

From looking at original pictures, of course some very slight details are missing due to the original stain this guitar was given. The main details though are exactly where they should be. The colour today is more natural or tea coloured than the original tinted orange. Also, some flecks of black lacquer are still in the grain when looking close up in parts. The contour toward the edges are remarkably flat which enhances the flat sawn grain pattern really well in the light. I have seen a picture of Bolan's roadie Mickey Marmalade bringing out this guitar for a photo shoot. He has the back of the guitar facing the camera and there is a curve in the grain in the centre of the mahogany just visible. Damage can be seen today near the edge of the binding above the strap button that indicates this guitar was dropped in more recent times. The Bigsby B7 holes are still visible and were a factory option that Gibson would fit. The binding around the body measures' 5.24mm/³⁄₁₆″ wide, the strap buttons are non original to this guitar. The weight is a very comfortable 8.44lb. Taking the control cover plate off reveals familiar details of this iconic guitar. It has clearly had the solder removed from the centralabs pots and the re-soldering from previous re-sprays was not done very well. Having said that, it was incredible to see after everything that has happened to this guitar they were

There has been much speculation down the years about when this guitar was built; many believe it was a goldtop from 1957 that was stripped. I take out the tone control on the bridge pickup to read the seven digit code along the side of the can, wow! Although it should only be used to determine approximate date of a guitar, other factors need to line up to give the year. The number is 1345947; this would mean the pots are from centralabs made November 1959! When added to the fact that this guitar has a Zebra PAF pickup in the neck position when Gibson reportedly ran out of black pigment, this pickup certainly fits in with the pot codes. They work perfectly; a curious note to mention here is that in a fan club magazine Q&A around 1972, Bolan said incorrectly that his Les Paul was a 1947 model and was the same age as himself! Of course this is wrong as they were not made until 1952. What struck me though are the last two digits on that centralabs number, he may have been told by a luthier at the time of one of his neck breaks that he thought the guitar was made in 1947. Let's not forget this at a time before internet or even any books out on the subject that could give you information.

serial numbers or pot codes might be the year of manufacture! Bumble Bee Sprague caps are fitted which I think are the best Gibson used. There are a few bits of solder which have been lacquered over, also evidence of black lacquer can be seen as well as some red which, judging by the look of it, is a nod to its a original sunburst colour. This red can be seen on the edges of the control plate screw holes as well as the toggle switch cavity just inside and the outer rim. The pickup surrounds are non original and the owner gives permission for me to take off the pickup cover to have a look at the zebra PAF. Lifting the pickup out and carefully unsoldering the cover, I gently squeeze it off. This pickup has survived well considering for most of its life it has not had a cover fitted, the PAF sticker is missing, but on the double white PAF the sticker is still in place. Inside the neck pocket you can see the neck tennon which does not look correct. There is also damage around it and a piece of wood has been put in on the treble side, probably as a result of the sheer number of necks that have been fitted, black paint and much epoxy glue is clear to see. It's also worth mentioning that on the outside heel where the neck joins the body, there is a crack that runs from the joint into the lower part of the body. I think when the neck broke the first time; damage must have cracked this area. If you look at photographs from around 1971 you can see the black lacquer extends further from the neck joint than it should to hide what I think would be the large crack.

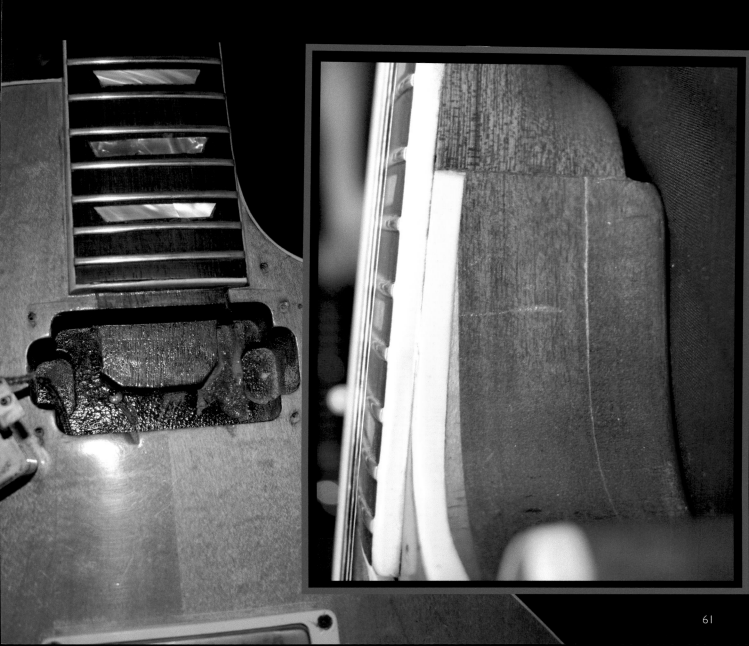

I could never work out where Bolan got the two Gibson custom necks from as in those days it was not easy getting these from America quickly, especially the first one. Maybe Bolan cannibalised a couple of second-hand customs and got them in repair fast. The pickup surrounds have had extra screw holes next to where they are today. Looking at th time the first Gibson custom neck was fitted it can be seen that this neck went in slightly further than it should, you can see in pictures that it is pushing and bending the front pickup surround which eventually broke and was changed.

The scratch plate is missing but purely to give it the look of how the guitar was when Bolan used it I put one in place on the guitar. I also put on a dummy (super thin) double black bobbin pickup with just the top showing, and also a zebra one which I placed on to of the covers. It's been an absolute thrill to see this old guitar after all these years and to be reminded of the many hits it has played on. The energy, originality and raw power produced by Marc Bolan and T. REX continue to influence many bands. Picasso said "art can't be explained adequately in words, because its influence on people is so personal an speaks to the nonverbal parts of our existence. Therefore art is an experience."

This guitar is functional art, and the sound it has produced has left a lasting legacy. Huge thanks to the owner for granting permission to examine this iconic guitar.

Present day mock up using old parts to show how the guitar looked in 1970.

tracks.co.uk

63

The guitar how it was originally in 1970

Hank Marvin/Bruce Welch 1959 Fender Stratocaster

There cannot be many guitarists especially in the UK over the last 50 years or so that have not been inspired by the Shadows to pick up the guitar and play. Pete Townshend, Eric Clapton, Jeff Beck, Ritchie Blackmore, Jimmy Page, Brian May, etc, all site them as an influence, but the guitar used by Hank Marvin set the tone for what was referred to as The Shadows sound. The group formed in 1958 as a backing band for Cliff Richard. Soon the song' Move It' was recorded which charted at number two in the UK even though the group did not play on it. The next song the band recorded was Living Doll plus tracks for the Serious Charge soundtrack/EP. In early 59, Shadows guitarist Hank Marvin was promised by Cliff that he would buy him a good guitar, as the Antoria LG50 he was using had a terrible neck. True to his word Cliff instructed a man called Dave Lilley by letter to buy Hank a Fender Stratocaster directly from America. At this time there was an embargo on foreign goods and Fender didn't have a distributer in the UK. They contacted Fender for a catalogue and when it arrived they couldn't believe how futuristic the guitar looked and were amazed. Both Hank and Bruce were huge fans of Buddy Holly and ordered a top of the line guitar with gold parts, in a Fiesta red colour with bird's eye maple neck finishing the look they wanted. The guitar was delivered to the flat that both Hank and Bruce shared at 100 Marylebone High Street London. This was one of the purportedly first ever maple necked Stratocasters in the UK.

Around July 1959, the Strat started to appear with a rosewood fingerboard. The neck on this guitar that Cliff bought had a wonderful bird's eye maple front and back, which was stunning to look at. According to Bruce Welch, the guitar was ordered based solely on a picture in the Fender catalogue (which he showed me later) rather than coming from a product listing. It has taken many months to track down Bruce, with false leads along the way and record company personnel having no contact information. After a conversation with a trusted colleague, I was given a clue on where to find Bruce, two telephone calls later, I got him! I introduce myself and try to give an idea of what I do. I never gave any thought really about the task at hand: it would make me too nervous. Anyway I tell Bruce that I'd like to measure the guitar in detail: that I would also like to take the guitar apart and then I held my breath, as did Bruce. After a pause he said " did you say take it apart hmmn...I will have to think about that so call me in a couple of weeks as I'm going away until then". Two weeks later I call and sure enough Bruce remembered our conversation but declines a full strip down of the guitar. But he does agree to a detail measurement and pickup DC check, which was fantastic news. After making travel arrangements I finally meet up with the man himself. When I arrive Bruce suggested we go get some lunch, this was a great idea I think for both of us!

We talked of course about guitars and gigs and Bruce's great admiration for Buddy Holly. He tells me that it was Lonnie Donegon who made Hank and Bruce want to pick up the guitar. He also spoke kindly of Jet Harris describing how inventive he was as well being the guy who came up with the name The Shadows. At the time there was an American outfit using their first choice of name The Drifters. Walking down the street with one of your guitar heroes can be a bit daunting but Bruce is never short of conversation, he is very enthusiastic to talk about what influenced him and it temporarily takes your mind of the fact that I'm about to examine Hank Marvin's guitar. It is claimed to be the first ever maple neck Fender Strat to arrive in the UK. The post world war 2 import trade ban on US goods, made getting a Fender instrument next to impossible for UK artists in the late 50s. Back at the arranged meeting place, it was good to get out of the heat, as this just happened to be the hottest day of the year so far. Once inside Bruce shows me some memorabilia and black & white photographs of Cliff Richard with the Shadows. One photograph showed Bruce holding a Grimshaw SS Deluxe in white: it looked really good and he started to reminisce about where it might be today. Then he brought in this beautiful flamingo pink Fender Strat.

Over the years a myth evolved that the guitar was Fiesta Red but Bruce has always maintained the guitar was more of a pink colour and this was also backed up by comments from Hank Marvin when Bruce was having the guitar restored to its original colour. "This is the 'Apache' guitar, Cliff paid 140 guineas for it so technically it's still his" he says! He told me the neck date says April 59, and looking at the back of the guitar we have serial number 34346 stamped on the neck plate. He mentioned that the G pole piece on all three pickups is pushed down flush and nobody knows why, as that's how it arrived in 1959. Bruce has a replica of it made by Fender in 2009 and the prototypes were made from the original and as Bruce would not let the guitar leave the UK, Fender came to him. Fifty four guitars were made and 50 were sold to the public whilst four were retained: Hank has number 51 which he took back to Australia and Bruce has 52. The Shadows manager was down for number 53 which Hank can make use of when he's in the UK. There will be no prizes given for guessing who has the fourth guitar!

I was given permission to examine the guitar as agreed, and Bruce said I could take as much measurement as I needed. I start off with the headstock which comes in at 14.35mm/⁹⁄₁₆" at the top for thickness. Machine heads are the original gold Kluson and work fine for this old guitar, the buttons are 17.46 across. There is some wear and slight lacquer cracking in this area especially near the Fender logo but, no major dings. The nut is 42.24mm/1¹¹⁄₁₆" and has been replaced and very well cut, it's also well spaced across all strings. The bird's eye maple fingerboard is stunning as is the back of the neck. Frets are 2.12mm/¹⁄₁₆" and the refret is excellent: at the 12th fret the neck width measures 52.16mm/2¹⁄₁₆" and I can say that it's a very comfortable neck to play. I plug my guitar lead into the jack socket to get a DC resistance reading on the pickups. The bridge pickup comes in at 6.30 ohms, mid pickup is 5.75ohms and the neck is 6.16 ohms. The pickups are all original and it's interesting to see how they were balanced for output in their positions.

I take a measurement of the plastic pickup cover on the bridge which is 17.63mm/¹¹⁄₁₆″ width, and the length is 69.60mm/2¾″. They are in very good condition with just slight wear as expected on the bass side edge. The control knobs are also original and in excellent condition. The diameter on the shaft lower point above the numbers is 17.74mm/¹¹⁄₁₆″ and the three-way switch tip at the lowest part is 8.68mm/¹⁄₃₂″. Although this guitar has been played over the years it has not been abused. It has been well looked after which is evident in the gold plating which is still intact on the machine heads and bridge. The only visual body damage is on the lower half of the guitar near the jack socket; there are a couple of chips in the lacquer and a large dent. When Bruce came back into the room I asked him what happened to the vibrato arm. He tells me he's not seen it for years as he does not use it. He then offered to go and look for it in some boxes full of Shadows memorabilia. About ten minutes later he arrives pleased that he had found it, so was I! I was told Hank made it shorter for his style of playing and cut it. But in an interview with Hank Marvin he said he didn't have anything initially to compare the vibrato arm with but, he noticed that some of the Fender Stratocaster's he saw seemed to have longer arms. Personally I cannot see how Hank took the plastic tip off without some damage being evident and the gold plating on the arm today although worn is not scratched.

The arm is slightly shorter than you would expect but great to see it back on this wonderful guitar again. The guitar weight of 7.28lb is a very comfortable area to be. I took a weight once of a 1979 3 bolt strat and it was almost 9.5lb. The body thickness at the top horn is 44.95mm/1¾", at the lower horn 44.81mm/1¾" and near the tone control it comes in at 43.85mm/1¾".

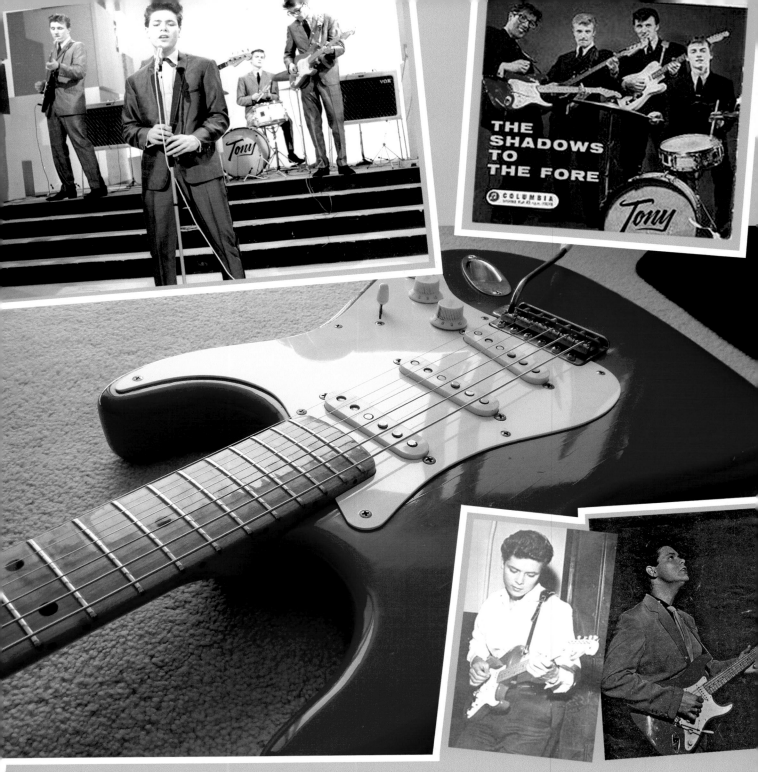

The bridge has quite a bit of gold plating left on it as do the saddles; the bridge length is 83.43mm/3¼". As my time comes to a close, I thank Bruce for his permission to examine this historic guitar as he clearly must know what it means to me. He said "you know what, I still get that excitement of what it was like for me and Hank when we first set eyes on Buddy Holly playing his Strat, it never has left me". Just before I leave I tell him that as a child I saved up my pocket money to travel into central Manchester England to buy a song book by The Shadows called The 5th album of guitar favourites: I had brought it with me to show him. I said I was disappointed that when I got home: not only were the chords wrong in the book but I didn't sound like Hank Marvin! He said the books were very successful but laughing he said the chords were wrong because they were transcribed in those days on piano. Nowadays all these secrets are revealed in countless YouTube videos with technical aspects of chords and of Hanks style to work out. What a great day this has been, thanks Bruce.

Bruce Welch with the Strat!
(June 2018)

Eric Stewart/Mick Ralphs Les Paul TV 1959

The Les Paul Junior was introduced in 1954 with a dark brown-over yellow lacquer giving intense shading on this entry/student model guitar. Les Paul and Mary Ford were extremely popular stars of the day and had their own TV show between 1954 and 1958 and even featured in TV commercials said to be shown up to five times a day, which in those days was massive TV exposure. Apparently the TV model was a sales idea to launch the guitar and a brilliant yellow finish was so the guitar would show up more effectively on black and white television sets! The colour was known as 'limed mahogany'. In late 1958 a double cutaway was introduced to give easy access to the frets above the 17th. A dark cherry red finish was now the chosen colour for the Junior models and soon after, a two pick-up special model appeared. The TV model now had a brighter yellow version of the earlier limed mahogany guitar. However, because of the difficulty producing the brighter yellow, some models varied in colour from creamy beige to a pale milky yellow. Sometimes this is due to the colour variants of the base mahogany and in other instances, depending upon where the guitar has been stored, it can be caused by exposure to ultra violet light.

The guitar sits in a Challenge #115 alligator soft shell brown case near a bright light from a nearby window. It was a sight to behold with its intense yellow finish: as you would expect of a guitar that's been around since 1959 it isn't too shiny. The checking in the finish is evident as the fine cracks in the lacquer completely cover the guitar. The weight of the guitar is 7.30lbs. Inside the case is a fine selection of additional parts including Grover USA machine heads, Kluson Deluxe machine heads, a Badass Bridge and interestingly, a Badass Bridge with brass saddles that numbered underneath 1-6 and finally two gold barrel speed knobs which appears to be the hardware used when Eric Stewart owned this guitar.

A Honduras Mahogany body and neck with unusually dark Brazilian rosewood fingerboard in surprisingly good condition. In the first three frets there is not too much wear and there is no binding on the neck, the dot inlays really set off the look of this guitar beautifully. Strangely enough I don't think crown inlays would look right on a guitar like this, maybe it is because it is quite stripped back in the hardware department and I guess the cost would have been a factor for Gibson also.

These are the parts that were on the guitar when Eric Stewart owned it.

It has a crack at the back but it's not serious. the yellow lacquer has worn through to expose the wood underneath but it is nice and smooth. The front headstock has very thinly applied black lacquer with plenty of dings and scratches but no checking cracks. The Gibson gold script logo is in good condition and again to keep costs down there was no pearl logo in there that you'd expect to see on the higher end Gibson's.

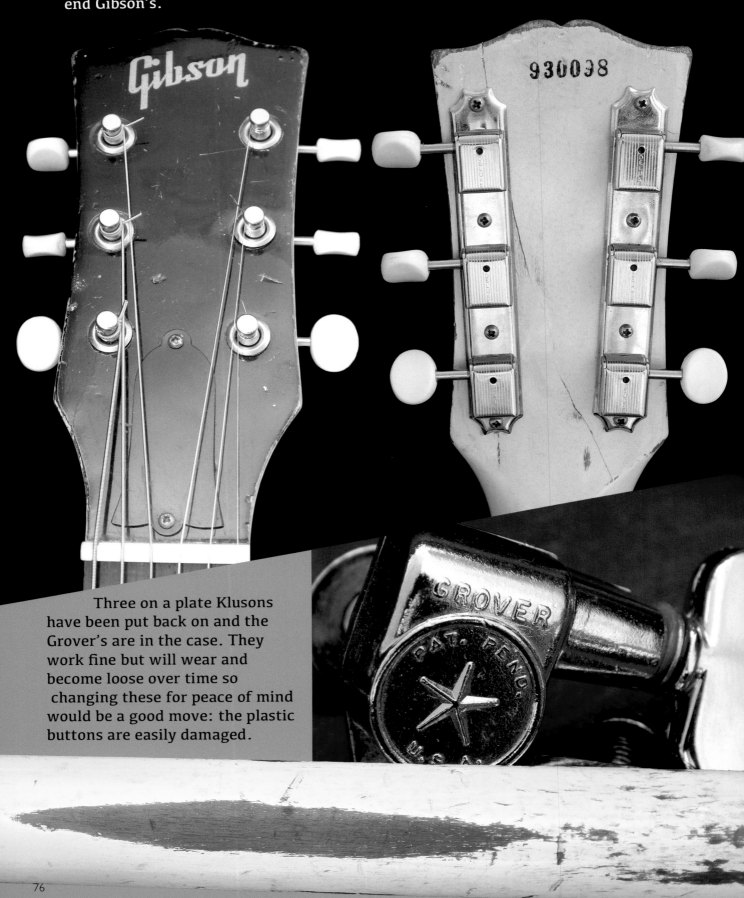

Three on a plate Klusons have been put back on and the Grover's are in the case. They work fine but will wear and become loose over time so changing these for peace of mind would be a good move: the plastic buttons are easily damaged.

The nut is 43mm/1¹¹⁄₁₆″ and made of bone although nicely cut in their slots, they are just a little too deep for maximum tone. Again this is an often overlooked area but its accuracy is essential for good intonation. Medium oval and well re-fretted and the fret ends are nicely finished with no sharp edges all the way up to fret 22. There are no dead spots to be found.

The neck has a good round feel, not too big. I once had a '59 Special that had a HUGE neck by comparison. When you take the pick guard off, you can see just how far the neck actually goes into the body giving great stability and transfer of sound. When Gibson added another pickup to the Les Paul Special, the joint was not so good and compromised the sound somewhat. It is clear that '59 necks on these guitars are not all the same. I've recently repaired a neck break on a Les Paul BFG and that was bigger at the back than the neck on this TV. I prefer the Les Paul TV neck for comfort: it's one of those guitars you don't want to put down: it makes you want to play and riff away all day. The pickup and cover are non-original and the current one has come off a Les Paul Special sometime in the past I am told, probably to suit the needs of the player at that time I'd guess. Les Paul Special P90 pickups are fairly consistent at around 8 ohms.

The control cavity reveals where there was a cut in the wire to join the pickup. But the way these pickups are mounted is also a significant factor in giving this guitar its distinct voicing and individual growl. The fact that the pickup is screwed directly to the wood will also affect the sound including the large pickup cover that will pick up subtle vibrations from the wood and transfer it back through the pickup. Unlike a Humbucker, which is basically floating in a chamber supported by a surround, the contact would be missing.

The wrapover bridge/tailpiece is nickel plated with small adjustable screws for intonation. It is anchored down by two stud screws. The fact that the strings are pulled over it again helps a lot with the voicing and the tone generated by this very simple design. Some players prefer to do a similar thing on Les Pauls with Tune-o-matic bridges by pulling the strings over the stud tailpiece first. Gibson actually did this on many of their guitars with this kind of set up but it wasn't consistent. There is an intonation compromise with this type of anchor, it is slight and if, as in this case, the nut has been cut as well as this one has, then the trade off is worth it. There is a single Sprague Bumble Bee cap fitted with a single 500k volume and single tone pot that each work perfectly. The tone control has a really nice smooth taper to give just a little more tonal interest. I remember some early '70's Les Paul Custom tone pots could be the 'all or nothing' types and I used to leave mine full on, but on this TV model I would definitely use it more often.

When the pickup was changed, the wire has been cut and rejoined to the original wire rather than soldered.

Plugging into the Cornell Plexi 18/20 Combo, the first thing that hits you is how loud it is even at low volume. When you play soft, all the dynamics are there until you play a bit harder and then it seems to reflect your personal style. There is such a honk with P90's that you don't get with Humbuckers, mid range is evident without it being muddy or lacking in clarity. The treble isn't high when compared to a Humbucker but the fullness of tone generated here is what grabs you. The guitar is very comfortable to play and well balanced too with easy access to the higher end of the fingerboard and the excellent re-fret with the low crown frets make it a joy to play.

Looking at the different bridges, pickup changes and machine heads used for each players' needs this guitar has been a work horse used to great effect. Eric Stewart has been a long underrated guitarist with an incredible vibrato: just listen to those early 10CC tracks and hear some fantastic riffs Eric played alongside Lol Creme. Mick Ralphs on the other hand as a player with a liking for Les Pauls', it is no surprise he found favour with this P90 loaded guitar. When cranked up, this guitar gives a lovely buzz saw sound that expresses beautifully, chords that are harmonically rich and lasting. The simplicity of construction in no way makes this a lesser guitar tonally and in my view it has plenty to offer any guitarist with a creative, expressive style.

Eric Stewart from the UK band 10CC co-wrote with bass player Graham Gouldman some of the bands biggest hits including I'm not in Love, Art For Art's Sake and Wall Street Shuffle. This Les Paul TV guitar was used by Eric during live work. He later sold it to Mick Ralphs, founder of Bad Company with singer Paul Rodgers from Free. The hit Can't Get Enough and 'Feel Like Makin' Love launched the bands success and Mick Ralphs use of the Gibson Les Paul became a crucial element of their sound.

I'm Not In Love
by ERIC STEWART and GRAHAM GOULDMAN

10 cc

The who

Pete Townshend (Eric Clapton Signature Strats)

On the eve of The Who's British Summer Time Show at Hyde Park, I am granted exclusive access to every inch of their live rig.

This is Pete's Torino Red strat (number 4) that he has been using since 1989. He has 4-6 more of these and all are Eric Clapton Signature models. There are numbers on the back of each guitar to say which one Pete would use during the set and for capo use. A Peterson Strobe Sensor 5000 Tuner is in front of us, it utilises an intuitive layout to accurately measure each scale note with unsurpassed precision, no pitch pipes here: this is serious tuning tech for the big boys! A small Vox amp with an 8" speaker is used to plug the guitar into. Pete's guitar tech, Alan Rogan tells me that Pete now uses 10 – 48 Ernie Ball RPS Slinkys. Alan removes the bottom 46 and replaces it with a 48 which he says Pete prefers.
    The guitar is basically a stock Eric Clapton model except for a Fishman power bridge fitted with a volume control that sits behind the treble side of the bridge: this controls the output of the piezo transducer saddles-pickup for acoustic sound. It's a stereo output that goes to a Pete Cornish splitter box that has the gold lace-sensor pickups from the guitar mixed with it.

On the back of the guitar is an EMG pre-amp which will boost the signal from the acoustic side that goes direct into the board. This combination provides an unbelievably good sound with such a punch and acoustic clarity: it's the best you can get. Out front near Pete's monitor there's a switch conveniently labelled 'Big Fat Switch' which enables him to shift between the sound combinations. The EMG pre-amp is adjustable and accessible through the back of the guitar using four trim pots and a three-band EQ and a volume.

This guitar has a 42mm/1¹⁰⁄₁₆ nut width and the slots for the strings have been impeccably cut as you would expect. On the top horn of the guitar I see many scratches on the surface where Pete would play most of his fast rhythm parts. The body is made of Alder and the gold lace-sensor pickups deliver a mid-range emphasis with a resistance of 5.8k complimenting the Fishman piezo perfectly.

The finish of the guitar is called a thin skin nitro cellulose lacquer which allows more resonance and adds great acoustic quality. The bridge width is 52mm/2$\frac{1}{32}$" on two pivot screw posts with two trem springs at the back. The scale length is 648mm/25½" with 22 frets with Sperzel locking machine heads. The first prototypes (1986-87) had 21 frets plus 21db boost and the first generation Eric Clapton Signature Strats that were introduced around 1988 had Gold Lace Sensors. The trem is set for a semitone pull back and the action is perhaps high for many strat players but for Pete's playing technique and power you wouldn't want it any lower. Once Alan has pre-stretched the strings and after locking them, he then tightens the machine head screw to keep things tight! The strings are not cut after passing through the machine head string posts until the next day's final tuning has taken place. Early versions of Pete Townshend's EC strats had a Kahler locking trem but now everything looks a lot tidier: never did like the locking nut stuff.

This is about as high as
Townshend's volume ever goes!

The frets have a little wear on them but don't need a fret dress. The bridge saddles on the Fishman have the top E saddle the lowest with the B saddle slightly higher than would be expected with the G and D set the same. The A is set lower with the bottom E slightly angled: it is quite interesting looking at this layout because it reflects the style and feel of the player. I notice that from about the 17th to the 22nd fret area that the edge of the maple fingerboard is darker and has worn through where the pick will be hitting it in some of Pete's rhythm playing.

SECTION
G F 7
KING'S HALL, BELLE VUE

HARVEY GOLDSMITH for John Smith Entertainments by arrangement with TRINIFOLD LTD. presents
THE WHO
plus Guest STEVE GIBBONS BAND

MONDAY
OCTOBER **6**
at 7-30 p.m.

GRAND
£2·00
Incl. VAT
NO TICKET EXCHAN
THIS PORTION TO B

KING'S HALL — BELLE VUE
FRIDAY 2nd NOVEMBER at 7.30 p.m.
John & Tony Smith in association with Five One Producti
present
THE WHO
IN CONCERT
plus
SUPPORTING ACT

Balcony Seat
CO./R EDINBURGH
No. **478** 2

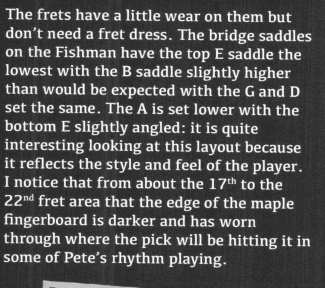

BLOCK 210
UPPER TIER   ROW   M SEAT   10
27-27991
                AMP & TRINIFOLD PRESENT
CLARKE/MRS   ** THE WHO **
£29.00   GREATEST HITS LIVE
SC   JOE STRUMMER + MESCALEROS
£29.00   M.E.N. ARENA DOORS 6:00PM
                THU 02-NOV-2000 AT 7:30PM

ticketmaster
www.ticketmaster.co.uk

Book Online
www.ticketmaster.co.uk
08705-344-4444. 24 HRS - 7 DAYS

No Exchange
No Refund

VOLUME

The Candy Apple Red Strat that Pete used throughout the Quadrophenia and more tour

Next out of the drawer is a Candy Apple Red Strat with number 8 on the back: again an EC model with Gold Lace Sensors and five-way switch. It has the mid boost and TBX tone circuit and this one has the three ply pick guard w/b/w that was used on the 'Quadraphenia and More' Tour 2012/13. This number 8 strat was also used on the Dublin gig two nights before and it too has Pete's blood on the scratchplate and strings at the end of the fingerboard. The edge of the fingerboard at the bass side 19th fret has some wear but is not as worn as the Torino Red strat. Scratches are still evident on the lacquer above the neck pickup and the top edge of the guitar where Pete's arm would rest has some lacquer chips, but the guitar is actually in good condition considering the owners reputation!

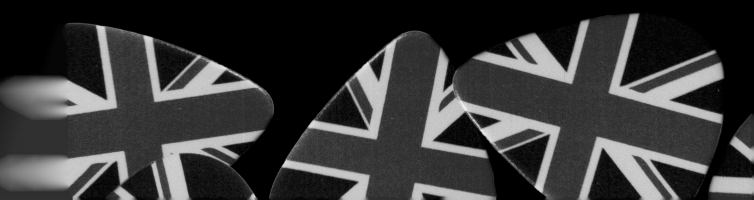

Sperzel locking machine heads with staggered tuning posts height are fitted with a butterfly string tree for the B and E strings. The G string chrome machine head has been changed or replaced and a satin finish machine head has been fitted. Some damage is evident on the headstock but it is not extensive.

Hyde Park, London
25th June 2015

Shoreline Gold Strat

Another EC model and has the same modifications with Fishman Power Bridge VMV (Vintage Mount Vibrato). Alan tells me that Pete has started using this one again after a short layoff. Interestingly, the last fret at the end of the fingerboard overhangs and you can see the tang under the fret wire as though it had not been trimmed when it was made. It is though in my opinion the best of the three guitars with no major dings although some surface scratches are visible. The trem, like the others looks set for a semitone pullback. The B string saddle is higher as on the other two strats. They all have the EC signature rubbed out because they are not EC models in the true sense any more. Alan makes a point of telling me that Pete pays for all his strats!

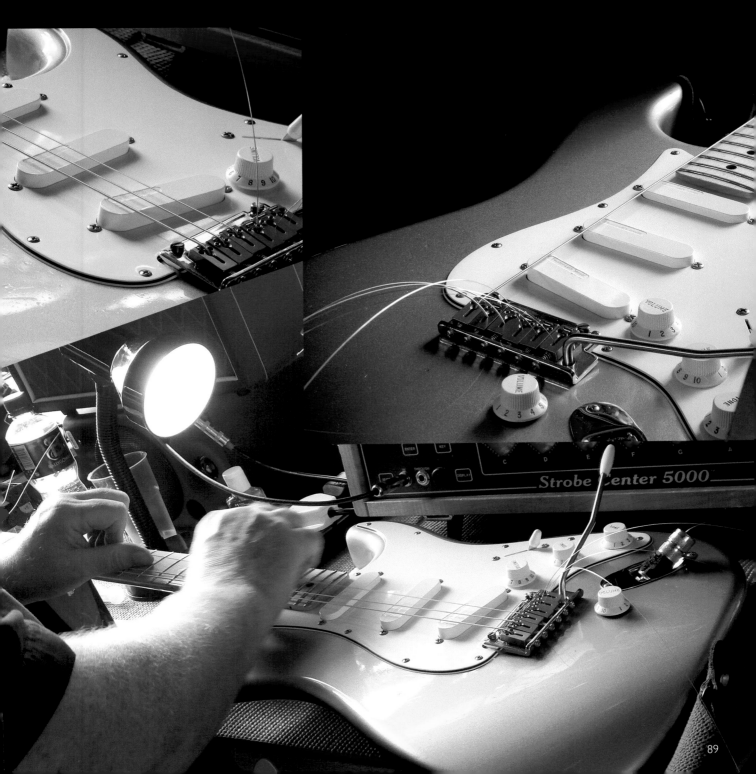

The Shorline Gold Strat has a Fishman Powerbridge VMV

Lace-sensor pickups have what is known as a radiant field barrier system that surrounds both the coil and magnets. The gold sensors read a greater physical area of the string whilst picking up less outside noise (50/60 cycle hum) so signal to noise ratio is phenomenal. The red sensor has the highest output of the lace series.

TubeTraps made by Acoustic Sciences Corp

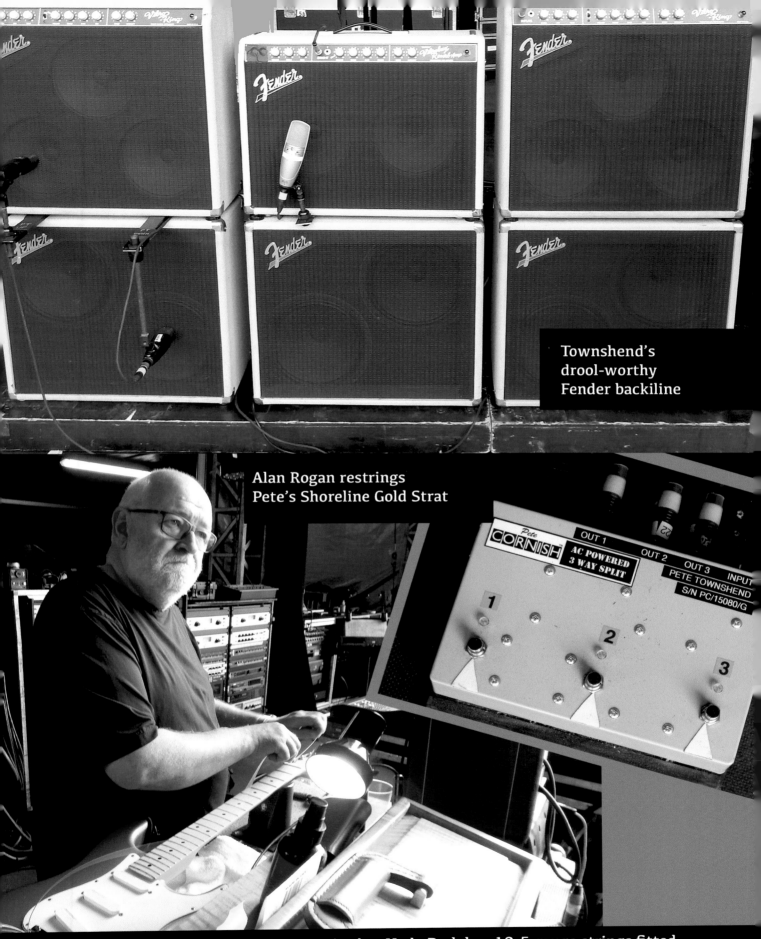

Townshend's
drool-worthy
Fender backiline

Alan Rogan restrings
Pete's Shoreline Gold Strat

Pete CORNISH
AC POWERED
3 WAY SPLIT
OUT 1   OUT 2   OUT 3   INPUT
PETE TOWNSHEND
S/N PC/15080/G
1   2   3

The black strat that fans may have noticed at Hyde Park has 10.5 gauge strings fitted
and is used for the song 'Love, Reign O'er Me' It is tuned half a step down. I didn't see
this guitar during my tour but Alan says he always has around 16 Strats ready and
waiting in the wings when The Who are on tour. A couple of them were custom made

Rickenbacker 1993 PT Fireglow 12-string

This is one of two Rickenbacker 12-string guitars that were sent to Pete. The colour is known as Fireglow and is stunning to look at and as I put my hand around the neck I note it has a really slim profile, especially around the first fret area. The model is called the 1993 Plus Pete Townshend 12-string which is an update of the model he had in 1993. The neck has been widened by 3.1mm/⅛" and the fingerboard is made from Caribbean Rosewood on a two-piece neck. It has three vintage reissue pickups and a stereo output and trapeze tailpiece that catches all twelve strings, this helps the tone as all the ball ends are touching each other.

When Pino was playing with The Who at Hyde Park 2015, his tech Michael Kaye shows me one of Pino's bass guitars; it's his own Fender Custom Shop Signature Bass. The bass has a lightweight Alder body that has a relic finish which is nitro cellulose. It has a C shape quarter sawn straight grain maple neck. The rosewood fingerboard has a scale length of 863.6mm/34" with a radius of 184.15mm/7¼" and a nut width of 44.45mm/1¾". There are 20 frets that are very well fitted with dot inlays: a vintage style split single coil precision bass pickup. It has a master volume and tone control with a four-saddle American vintage bass bridge, and the aged nickel/chrome hardware that has been oxidised looks great.The scratchplate is the four-ply tortoiseshell type and there are knurled flat top control knobs. There is a vintage style slotted truss rod nut and the aged plastic parts finish it off. This guitar is based upon a 62' relic Fiesta Red. The aged lacquer effect is extremely well done and has none of the circular scratch marks that can be seen on some relic models.

Michael Kaye – with Pino's bass pre gig Hyde Park, London 2015.

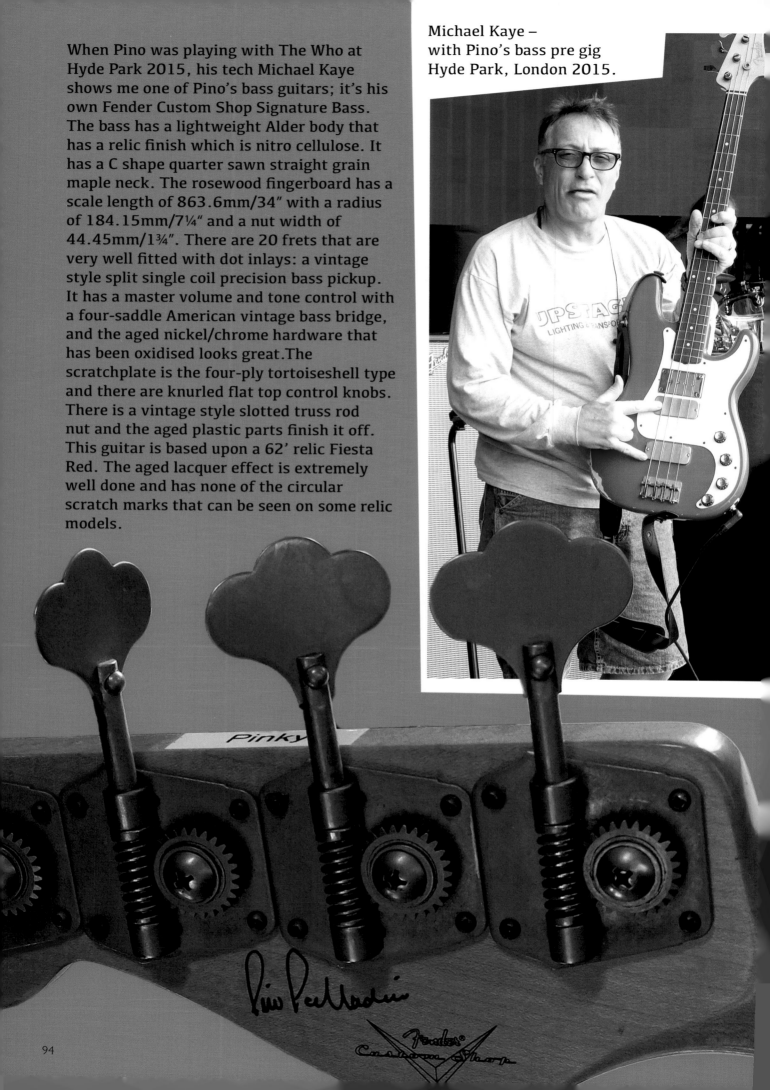

Pinky

Pino Palladino

Fender®
Custom Shop

Mike then shows me Pino's guitar rack and pulls out Pino's second bass. I notice straight away on the top edge of the headstock a white piece of tape with the word 'pinky' written on it. This model appears to have two old Thunderbird pickups fitted with stainless steel covers. He then takes me to another flight case and inside is a small soft case housing more effects, there is a Rumble Seat Drive delay reverb box that was recommended to both Pino Palladino and Simon Townshend by Joe Walsh, this one has three foot switches. Next to that, there is an Alien Bass Station, a Fuzz Bubble 45 and an Alien Twister Analogue Fuzz. Other effects are a DiscumBobulator which is an autowah by Emma Electronics, a Boss Octave, a channel switcher and a Snark tuner. Palladino uses Fender Super Bassman amps.

Pete Townshend's live guitar playing is a force of nature. His control over the wall of sound he creates is phonemenal, as is his command of dynamics wether he is playing a solo or arpeggiating in quick succession. And, when he hits that A chord, he does it like nobody else can. Alan Rogan is a vital link in Townshend's chain too, he has been Pete's tech for many years, and has a unique understanding of all that is required to keep his guitars in top shape,which in turn helps The Who remain one of the biggest live bands on the planet after more than five decades in the business.

The who↑

LIVE IN HYDE PARK

INCLUDES
10 PREVIOUSLY
UNRELEASED TRACKS
PLUS EXCLUSIVE
12 PAGE BOOKLET
273 429 5

Keith Richards/Mick Taylor Gibson Les Paul 1959 Standard

This guitar was used on the album 'Exile On Main Street' It has a Honduras Mahogany body and neck with a colour faded reddish orange, the years have been kind as there is no buckle wear as you might expect from a guitar of this pedigree, sure, there are plenty of knocks and dents but the lacquer on the back has held up well. The sides though have seen a lot more wear and tear. A hole surrounded by a faint circle on the back of the guitar indicates that a strap button had once been fitted. Originally a Bigsby was fitted on this guitar evidenced by two Bigsby holes at the tailpiece on the left and right sides. At some point in the past the nut has been replaced but this one measures 43mm/1¹¹⁄₁₆".

The neck is very comfortable to play. Typical of '59 Les Pauls, it has a small heel (most early 58's were larger). There are also signs that the neck has been refinished at some stage. There is though quite a bit of damage on the binding on the bass side of the first four frets and it has been replaced with a binding that is whiter than the original cream. It looks like the newer binding has been on quite a few years though as it is now beginning to age a little. The crown inlays are in good condition as well with no sign of damage or cracking. The rosewood fingerboard has started to wear around the G string 2nd fret and also around the top E 2nd fret and 3rd fret on the 2nd string. The frets are the Jumbo type but obviously done some time before the guitar was sold to the current owner as there is very little wear on them even considering the current owner has had the guitar for 30 years.

The headstock has lost its Les Paul script and has also had a clear lacqler overspray, but the black underneath is original. All the scratches and marks are actually underneath the clear lacquer so we know it hasn't had a total refinish. Machine heads are Grover but there is another set of Grovers in the case that early pictures of the guitar indicate were on first. Originally though, this guitar would have had Kluson machine heads with a single ring on the plastic tulip button and you can see clearly from the holes on the headstock where they would have been. Curiously, the serial number has been scratched on as it was lost due to sanding when the neck had an overspray. The number originally would have been ink stamped and the current number 8R1652 doesn't make much sense when you first look at it. The second digit has been made to look like a letter R and the first looks like a badly scratched 8. There shouldn't be 6 characters in this serial number anyway although in late 59 and early 60, Gibson did fill the gap between the year and the remaining four digits as their high production at this time did reach 9.999. But I have never heard of an original Les Paul from '59 with a six digit serial number although other models did. In 1960 Les Paul's did appear with six digits beginning with 0.

It is highly unlikely that this guitar is a 58 Les Paul because the double cream PAF that this guitar has in the bridge was more common towards the latter part of '59. Is it possible that before the guitar had a refinish on the neck, the no. 9 in the serial number had a curling tail that looks like 9: easily mistaken for an 8, especially on a guitar with scratches and wear marks? With regard to the letter R, again before the refinish, the number would have been written down and post spraying, mistakenly etched on, the gap was filled in with an R for identification/fun to imply "Richards". Why make any effort to reinstate the number when leaving it blank is acceptable as you see on many refinished guitars. It doesn't make any sense to make the attempt without making a point. After searching many sites, books and Gibson's own factory ledgers (what was left after the fire) I can confirm that a Les Paul left Gibson's Kalamazoo factory with a serial number 9 1652. I can also confirm that there is no such Gibson serial number as 8R1652

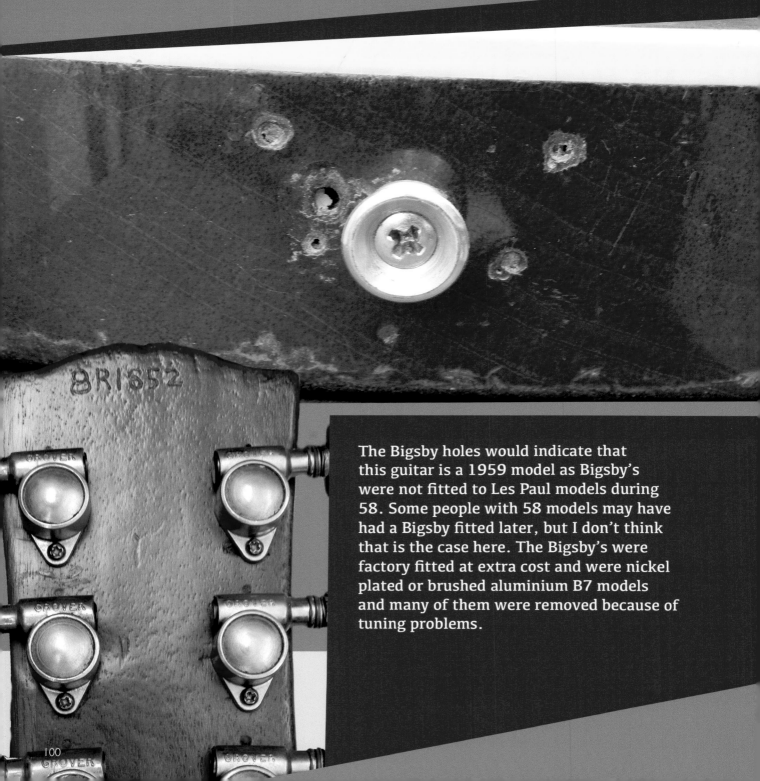

The Bigsby holes would indicate that this guitar is a 1959 model as Bigsby's were not fitted to Les Paul models during 58. Some people with 58 models may have had a Bigsby fitted later, but I don't think that is the case here. The Bigsby's were factory fitted at extra cost and were nickel plated or brushed aluminium B7 models and many of them were removed because of tuning problems.

Looking inside you can see some splashes of red dye from where the guitar would have had a stain put over the grain filler and has left its mark. The wiring seems quite neat except for the bridge volume pot which is a little untidy compared to the rest: the solder is generous. I could read the manufacturers code on all the pots, in this case 137. That means they were made by CTS (Chicago Telephone Service). The next digits are 690 and when I carefully used my finger to remove some grime I find a number 1 making the complete serial number: 1376901.

According to the company, this would mean it was made first week January 1969! This speaks volumes if you'll pardon the pun, because now we know that around this time or even 1970 maybe that this guitar had all the pots changed as they all code to the same date.

Keith Richards set list taken from the side of his monitor at Bell Vue Manchester UK in Sept 1973.

The owner told me beforehand that the covers on the guitar had already been de-soldered on the back. The cans were just squeezed over the bobbins for easy removal to see what was underneath. I started with the bridge pickup first, removing the very aged and dirty screws to see inside this famous time capsule. As soon as the last screw came out I carefully lifted the pickup out, realising that what I'd thought were nickel covers were actually gold plated covers underneath. This again throws up the possibility that even before Keith had the guitar, it may have had the cans removed as it was known that Eric Clapton and others removed them around 1968 and got people interested in doing the same. It would seem they were put back on though either before or when Keith Richards purchased it because early photos of the guitar show them in place.

The toggle switch nut assembly beneath the plastic tip is also gold plated but much the worse for wear. I carefully lifted the cover off which then exposed double cream bobbins, a classic sign that this guitar is from the period of late 1959. Double creams started to appear more at this time because the black carbon pigment used in the manufacturing process temporarily started to run out. The pickup resistance is 8.27ohms. Around serial number 9-1000 to 9-1100 zebra and double creams were more common. The classic 'Patent Applied For' (PAF) sticker was there underneath the pickup at the bottom of the plate and the black tape wrapped around the bobbins was nice and tight. Looking inside the cavity you can now see the half inch maple cap that gets thinner towards the edge of the guitar: the total thickness is around 57.1mm/2¼". The pickup surrounds are period correct and although very dirty, just visible underneath are M-69 markings. Having placed the pickup back it was now time to take a look at the neck pickup.

Again, carefully lifting this out, I could see once more what first looks like a nickel cover is actually another gold plated one. The pole piece adjustment screws are also very dull and dirty but it definitely has gold plating around the edges unlike the bridge pickup which does not. The other noticeable difference was the absence of the PAF sticker which may have been lost at a time when somebody has handled the pickup. After removing the cover I find this time double black coils with lots of dirt and corrosion around the pole pieces. The magnet is long and one of the bobbins has a small square within a circle indicating that this is actually a period PAF. In 1961 it changed to a short magnet for the whole production of pick-ups at that time. The braided wire coming out of this has a blob of solder and a bit of clear tape around it suggesting it had been cut when the pickup was replaced: the pickup measures 7.49 ohms. The spacing on the pole pieces indicates that the pickup has probably come off a jazz type guitar such as a 355, 345 or a Birdland etc. Keith Richards did use a 1959 Gibson 355 in 1969 and although generally black Les Paul Customs all had the same pickup spacing, I've seen two '57 customs with front pickup jazz guitar spacing, both Mick Taylor and Keith Richards used three pickup customs and Keith did have four at one time. Is it possible that they were serviced at the same time as this standard and parts were swapped about? It would explain the gold in the front and rear pickup cans, bridge thumbwheels and toggle nut....who knows? Inside the cavity, the neck tenon is now clearly visible and everything is cut nicely, which is testament to the people at Gibson who built this guitar with loving care. Also it is extremely rare for one of these joints to ever fail.

Taking a weight of the gutiar, it comes in at just under 8.5lbs. The guitar has an ABR1 Tune-o-matic Bridge fitted but non original, also in the case was another no-name bridge. Bridge adjustment wheels are gold plated though as opposed to the nickel that you would expect. Interestingly both have retaining clips that shouldn't be there. Also in the case was a spare tailpiece, non original too. Other goodies in the case was a toggle switch cap that looks like it could be the original, before the current one was fitted along with a set over Grover copy type machine heads. How fantastic to have such historical parts from such a well photographed guitar.

  The tailpiece fitted on the guitar is non-original although nickel plated. The studs which anchor it down are clearly chrome and would not be original either. Let's not forget, we are talking of a workhorse of a guitar for the Rolling Stones and if something didn't look right to the eye, maybe like corrosion, they had a plentiful selection of other guitars to pick and choose new parts from.

Well, what can you say about a guitar that both Keith Richards and Mick Taylor played when touring and recording, especially the latter part of Exile on Main Street and the 1972 American Tour. Although both guitarists used this guitar, the original finish is in surprisingly overall good condition. The typical checking you get on a guitar of this age is evident on the top of the maple and especially around the treble pot. Unbelievably, the upper part of the guitar has not worn through the lacquer where the arm would rest and has retained its colour which has faded to a lovely shade of golden amber, except for the red that is still near the toggle switch area and cutaway. When I took the scratch plate off you could see just how much of the original red was still remaining.

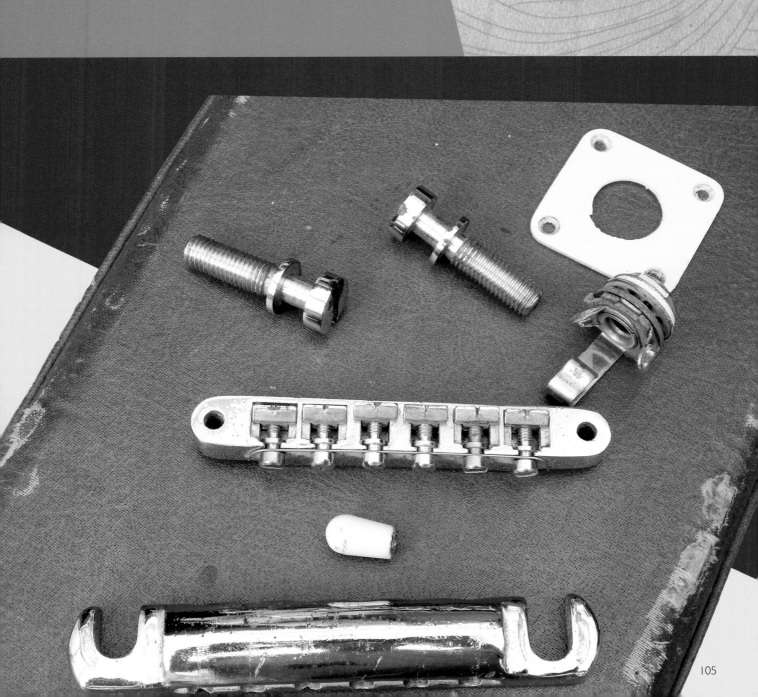

Just checking the toggle switch cavity at the back reveals a Switchcraft with white powdery deposits along the top edge but it does not affect in any way the performance: it's really just where a micro-climate has existed over the years. Looking deeper into the cavity I can see some chipping away of the maple at the bottom where the switch comes through. The switch is nickel in colour all over, it is only on the outside that the threaded nut is gold.

How do you describe a sound? Well I'll do my best. I plugged into an original Marshall Bluesbreaker combo which was perfect. I set the amp not too loud and relatively clean and flicked to the bridge pick up first. Considering the strings aren't new there is an immediate well-balanced sound with a beautiful harmonic mid-range that seems to fade in as the chord I play dies away. The treble frequencies are all there without sometimes the harshness or spike you can sometimes get when you hit hard. Listening to an F chord, the bottom E string is not swamping the rest of the strings, although the owner did allow me to tweak the pole pieces to enhance everything. This is a beautiful sounding pickup and again proves that overwound hot pickups are not the place to be in the search for tone. Putting the toggle in the middle position activates both pickups and because the front pickup is slightly lower in output, there is not the overwhelmingly thick rhythm sound you would expect. Instead the notes become very defined, a bit like you have just boosted the frequency of each string without it being too muddy: I really like this! It is such an expressive tone and one I personally would not use much on a Les Paul but with this kind of balance I would. Another thing that I like with the middle position on this guitar is the subtle sound you can achieve when you back off either volume and bring in more or less of either pickup. Flicking over to the neck pickup reveals another surprise in that my anticipation of huge bass and lots of low and mid was not that evident. But this was in no way a bad thing, because it still had enough guts and low end without again having to tame it a little by taking the pickup down in its surround for balance between the two.

I'm not a big fan of pickups that sound like they are on steroids when you use the toggle. Yes sure, there is room for that type of pickup on other guitars for certain music to be heard, but you just do not want that power on a classic Les Paul. Whoever changed this pickup wanted a certain voice to suit their own playing style that the original did not have. It was common practice late '60s early '70s to experiment like this with pickups: the range of floor pedals we have today did not exist to boost or tame your sound.

I am still reminded of what classic guitar sounds made me want to spend hours listening to riffs where you could hear the communication between player, guitar and amp.
The shift to digital proccessing provided us with a palette of sounds to inspire us with fantastic creative effects.
People like Peter Green, Gary Moore and now Joe Bonamassa have all allowed the expression of what they feel to translate through the guitar first. I personally still love the simplicity of the sound of guitar, amp and reverb. This guitar can be heard on Exile on Main Street to great effect and Mick Taylor can be heard playing some brilliant licks with the Rolling Stones Live. It is rare indeed to ever see a guitar of this calibre and pedigree these days, so to have the opportunity to get inside and up close to reveal the voice of this instrument has been a pleasure and privilege.

George Harrison 1956 Fender Stratocaster

Just as I was about to finish this book, I finally receive a call from the owner of this wonderful guitar who had given me permission to go with the detail that I had discovered that day on this special guitar. I am very grateful for his understanding, as it's not a decision taken lightly pulling apart this old Strat, especially one that's been played by George Harrison! This Strat was part of the production of the TV show in 1995 book (and video as was) The Story of the Fender Stratocaster, Curves Contours, and Body horns. Many big name players took part in this programme, including Keith Richards, Eric Clapton, Mark Knopfler and George Harrison for whom this guitar was used. There is a brief talk from George about his guitars and a clip of him playing this guitar on YouTube. George Harrison has played quite a number of guitars with his time in The Beatles, Gretsch guitars, Rickenbacker's, a 1968 rosewood Telecaster and a Les Paul named Lucy, named after the redhead actress Lucile Ball. This Les Paul he later gave to Eric Clapton who had played the solo on the song, While My Guitar Gently Weeps. George Harrison though has a strong connection with the Strat, and in 1965 he purchased a sonic blue Stratocaster at the same time John Lennon received his. They had a matching pair of 1961 Strats that were bought during the making of the album Rubber Soul; also the two guitars can be seen in the film Help, playing Ticket To Ride. One day during 1967 George stayed up late one night and decided to paint his Strat in Day-Glow paint; he also used his ex-wife's Patti Boyd's nail polish to paint the headstock. George Harrison is such an underrated player and his rhythm playing is remarkable, he just knows what's needed. This guitar is in very good condition, and the two tone sunburst looks amazing. I requested a bright room with some natural light as the fluorescent lights above me was not good for the pictures I was looking for. After re-locating to a much better room, the floor was ideal as the only table available had only three legs and was just about big enough to put a banjo on it!

rt by taking the pickgard screws off the guitar after removal of the strings, and ully lifting out the assembly. I am quite certain that these screws have never been his guitar before, there are tell tale signs and the amount of dirt and grime around the outer edge of the pickgard, inside has lots of dust and the screws are immaculate and have no previous attempt of removal. The nail holes are visible which was used to hold the body when being painted. Looking at the controls, the number stamped on the back of the volume pot reads 304605 made by stackpole Feb 1956.The large capacitor is known as a phone book type, a wax impregnated sealed unit to prevent moisture and corrosion. The solder joints look original on the controls and 3 way switch, the orange halo around the outer edge of the solder is very tidy indeed, a tell tale sign done long ago.

112

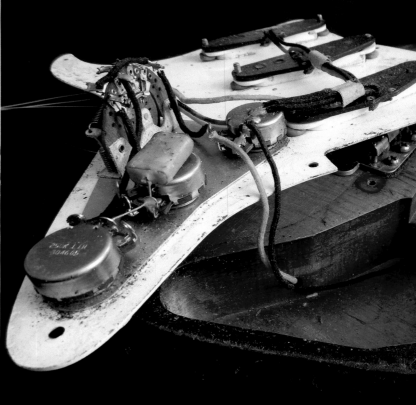

The control knobs are original and are the polystyrene type, often called Bakelite you can see the volume knob is slightly more round and smooth compared to the others. I take a measurement at the lower skirt which is 25.54mm/1″ and the grooved part above is 18.92mm/¾″ where it joins the numbers. The pickgard is made from ABS or vinyl used from 1954 to 1959 and again much grime is evident. The pickup covers are also made from polystyrene and the centre and neck show some ware but the bridge is still sharp, 69.42mm/2¾″ length and 17.56 mm/¹¹⁄₁₆″ width.

Next I take a DC resistance for the pickups at this stage and the Bridge comes in at 5.78 ohms, the middle is 5.63 ohms and the neck is 5.70 ohms. The bridge has held up well and measures 83.31mm/3¼" length, 38.85mm/1¹⁷⁄₃₂" width. The bridge saddles are 11.03mm/⁷⁄₁₆" width and are in very good condition.

Moving on to the body work, ash bodies were still used until around mid 56 when alder became the chosen wood to use depending on model and reissues. This two tone sunburst looks fantastic even though on the edge of the body there are lots of dents and scratches, and the lacquer is worn through. The body thickness is 44.57mm/1¾" on the upper horn and some ware is evident. The back of the body between the tremolo plate and the neck plate, the lacquer has worn through in the contour area. The neck has some dark patches along various points and especially at the end of the fingerboard, it is quite worn, also the round string retainer in place would soon give way to the butterfly type at the headstock. The back of the neck has some discolouration but good condition otherwise. The frets measure 2.06mm/¹⁄₁₆" and at the end of the fingerboard there is a pencil signature, X A and the date which looks like 4-56(April 1956). This signature is supposed to stand for Xavier Armenta the man who was responsible for signing the neck. It is also written at the end of Eric Clapton's Strat called brownie which he bought sometime in 1967 and went on to use for Layla.

The headstock thickness is 14.89mm/⁹⁄₁₆″ at the top edge; machine heads are single line Kluson deluxe and the nut measures 42.07mm/1⅝″ and at the 12ᵗʰ fret the neck measures 50.50mm/1³¹⁄₃₂″. The first fret thickness is 23.78mm/¹⁵⁄₁₆″ and 24.65mm/³¹⁄₃₂″ at the 12ᵗʰ fret. It's getting close to my time up with this fantastic Strat that George played so I start to assemble the guitar and put the strings back on it. I plug the guitar into a small Fender amp on a clean setting; the bridge has this lively springiness to it, not shrill or harsh like some later pickups could be. The mid position has an openness that responds to every note played with wonderful harmonics definitely not honky. The neck has no jump in volume in the bass and is beautifully balanced, in fact it's a joy to flick through these pickups and be rewarded with what these great Strats could deliver, and the playability is excellent. It is also such a resonant guitar even when not plugged in! The weight is taken and comes in at 7.52lbs. It's time for me to part with this guitar as security has just walked in; they are keen to get it back in the display in the Beatles memorabilia at the British Music Experience in Liverpool. It's been an absolute thrill to play and examine in detail such a guitar and I thank the B.M.E. and especially David Brewis the owner of this guitar of Rock Stars Guitars who runs rockstarsguitars.com and with US – based Greg Dorset.

Jan Akkerman – Les Paul Personal

The Les Paul Personal was introduced in late 1969 and the first prototype had a regular Les Paul sized body. It had the small fretless wonder frets which were not popular and they were soon replaced with Jumbo frets for ease of playing. It was built from a clear grain British Honduras mahogany body with a centre cross-band and dimensions of 463.55mm/18¼" long body, 355.6mm/14" wide and 50.8mm/2" thick. It had a three piece laminated mahogany neck that was quarter sawn for added strength. With a dark walnut finish, ebony fingerboard and mother of pearl block inlay, it also had gold plated deluxe sealed metal machine heads that were better than the plastic Kluson button type. At that time they cost more than the Les Paul Custom and were quite heavy at typically between 8.5 –12lbs. The total number shipped was only 146 between 1969 and the middle of 1971.

The early seventies was a period that many would consider a riff would be the start of any guitarist's obsession to emulate their chosen guitar hero. Many hours would be spent putting the needle on that vinyl record in the hope of finding where and how to play that elusive riff. In 1971 a Dutch group called Focus released the track 'Hocus Pocus' from the album Moving Waves, it did not chart until 1973 when a fast version of the recording was done. Anyone who remembers seeing them on the Old Grey Whistle Test TV show would not fail to note the incredible playing of the guitarist in the band called Jan Akkerman. He was using a black Les Paul Custom two-pickup model and from early pictures of this guitar with its 'Witch Hat' volume and tone knobs it looks like the post '68 reissue.Not longer after, Akkerman changed the front pickup to a Gretsch Filtertron and eventually another one was fitted in the bridge pickup position. He apparently wired it wrong and it was out of phase. None the less it started a lot of tongues wagging, mine included as to what was going on with this modification. Akkerman has never been afraid to try various combinations of pickup and wiring options and using custom made guitars in the quest for great tone. I visit Gilze Rijen, Holland, where I meet Peter Herwegh, the owner of Brandin Guitars. We go to the factory where the Les Paul Personal that Jan used in Focus has been brought for me to examine. Jan Akkerman used this guitar from around 1971 in Focus through to present day.

When I open the case Jan's beautiful looking guitar in two-tone dark burst is mesmerising. It is just stunning to look at and what strikes me is the shape: it has a more rounded lower horn than a Standard or Custom guitar and is slightly wider across the body. The condition is very good and where the XLR microphone socket at the top edge of the guitar would be, there is a filled repair with a well matched piece of mahogany. According to guitar builder Wim Heins who has worked on this guitar, it has been re-topped, re-necked, the headstock has been broken off several times and the electronics have been replaced too. A new two-piece flame maple top has been put on and it has a real three-dimensional look about it. The weight is 10.3lbs and it has three Humbucking pickups. In early 1973, Paul Hamer of Hamer Guitars was asked to take the low impedance pickups out and replace them with two Humbuckers. A wrapover bridge was fitted with two tone and two volume controls positioned slightly closer together than normal to facilitate Jan's technique of bowing: using his little finger to swell the note. With the body of the guitar being wider and larger it had more sustain than Jan's black Les Paul Custom even though it was lighter in weight. The binding has been replaced and the frets are jumbo sized, measuring 2.62mm/³⁄₃₂″. The fret wire runs to the edge of the board and sits atop the binding. This is something that Gibson now does on all of their new guitars except for vintage reissues. The neck is a very comfortable shape thats quite slim at the back and measures 53.4mm/2³⁄₃₂″ across the heel. The neck pickup is a Gibson 57' reissue and measures 7.86 ohms: these reissues were made to Seth Lovers original specifications and is closer to the original design. Because of the way they were made no two pickups have the same specs due to them being wound by hand leading to inconsistencies in output.

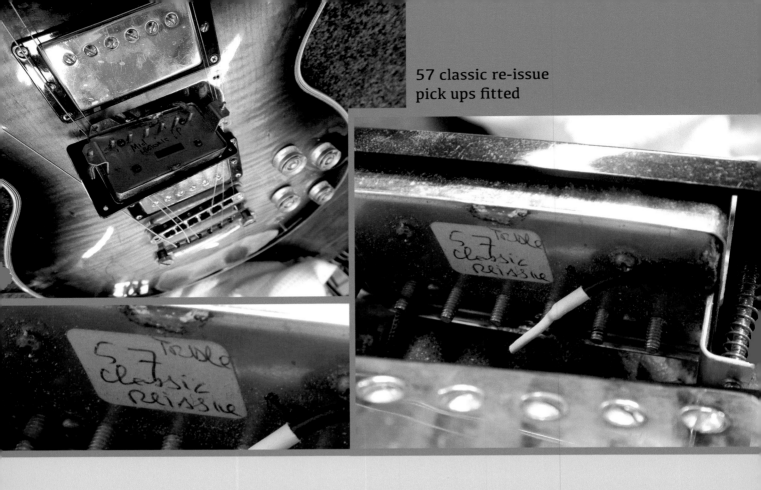

57 classic re-issue
pick ups fitted

The two coils of wire in each pickup were unbalanced, magnets changed over the years but the character of a 57' pickup is reproduced in this design. Alnico V magnets were used on the original pickups but the reissues use Alnico II, wax potted to cut down any squeal. Also two conductor braided wiring was used as can be seen in this case. The middle pickup which I take out has a PAF sticker on the bottom of the plate and black marker writing that says "mid historic PP." It has a DC resistance of 8.12 ohms. Lifting the bridge pickup out reveals a white sticker with "57 Treble Classic Reissue" written on it. There is a black wire coming from the underside metal plate with a white insulating cover which looks like a ground wire, as the braided wire is at the other end going into the control cavity. A small piece of sponge is underneath the pickup which could be there to stop movement as the springs are not that strong. The pickup resistance is 8.26 ohms. The routing for the pickups is very clean and neat but does not replicate Gibson shaped routing. The front pickup surround has "M69" stamped underneath and looks to be an original Gibson but the middle and bridge surrounds do not and you can see the edges of the plastic are serrated and not smooth indicating that they are from a different supplier. The toggle switch surround is gold plated with a metal switch tip and looks well suited to this great looking guitar.

The controls sit inside metal foil that completely shields the inside as well as the cover that is labelled "Wim Heins April 1998" which I remove. There is just one Gibson stamped volume pot and a CTS volume and two tone controls, but the lower bridge tone control is not connected to anything! The mini toggle switch gives a variety of sounds in conjunction with the main Switchcraft toggle switch, so really it has simply a master tone control and two volumes. The pot code that I can see reads EPO86 500 1017 CTS which tells me this pot was manufactured 17th week of 2010.

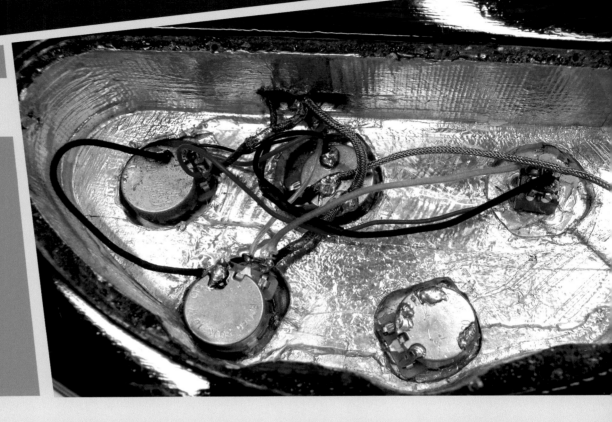

Control
cavity

You will see pictures of this guitar in its many guises but to summarise: in 1998 it had cream pickup surrounds and a Stets bar trem that was fitted by Marcus Van Engelen who was local to Akkerman. As his guitar shop was close to where Jan lived he was his "go to guy" for repairs and everything electronics. Marcus is quite the electronics wizard and as Jan always liked to tinker on his guitars it was a quite natural match that they met up and worked on his guitars. Later in May 2000 it is seen with three black surrounds and still had the split diamond headstock, bonnet knobs, tune-o-matic bridge and tailpiece and then in 2005 we see it with a mini toggle switch on the upper neck tone control and the headstock is plain.

Steve with Les Paul Personal

Original broken headstock

Later around 2010 Fred Dons put a mother of pearl inlay on the headstock depicting Akkerman holding a guitar which is extremely well done. The Gibson logo was done by Marcus Van Engelen.

Over the years there have been some changes here: originally they would have been deluxe sealed gears but later after Jan got the guitar, Grover Imperial Stairstep machine heads were fitted. These were possibly taken from a Gretsch, however the guitar today has generic gold plated locking machine heads. What is interesting is that the machine head buttons are not part of these locking tuners, I can see the same buttons (called Butter Bean) fitted on his Gretsch White Falcon, later they also appeared on his Les Paul Custom with two Gretsch pickups: are these the same ones? They feel great and your thumb fits in them perfectly. I prefer this mish-mash to the stock Grover types. Jan also uses 8's string gauge. Across the top of the headstock it measures 86.56mm/3¹³⁄₃₂" and the thickness from around the bottom E machine head area is 16.02mm/⅝" tapering to 14.05mm/⁹⁄₁₆" at the D string machine head. Wim Heins says that the original split diamond headstock that was broken had the serial number 906011. This guitar could be either late 69 or 70.

The bridge is non original and of a type that Gibson used from 1974 and of the Nashville style, what is curious are the threaded metal inserts that screw over the bridge posts and the bridge is then squeezed over the top sitting on two thumb wheels for a secure fit: this will help in tone transfer. The bridge saddles are made of graphite for less friction and are very smooth from wear and tear. The bridge width is 13.89mm/⁹⁄₁₆″ and the length is 85.45mm/3²³⁄₆₄″.

The bone nut measures 42.43mm/1⁴³⁄₆₄″, has a small gap on the treble side and has been cut very well and low at the first fret, but the wound strings sit a little lower than they should be which would reflect Jan's playing style. The wide spectrum of his technique especially the incredibly rhythmic parts he plays with his thumb could possibly result in the strings popping out if they sat higher up.

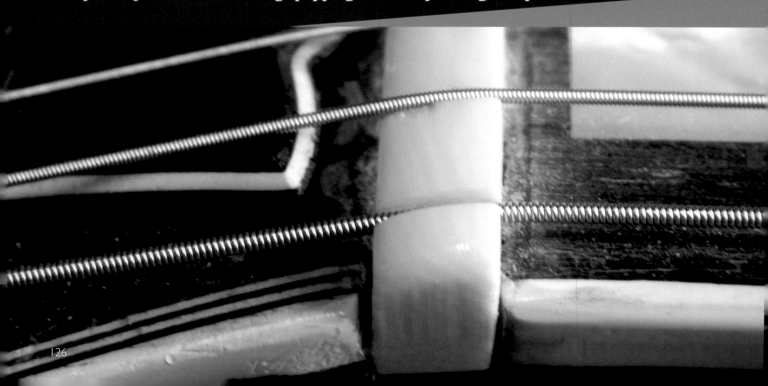

I am impressed with how well balanced the guitar is, I think the extra size distributes a good weight between body and neck. Starting with the front pickup with mini toggle in the mid position and the main toggle up, this is such a great tone with not a lot of bass boom that you sometimes get with neck humbuckers. The tone control really takes out all the treble with a smooth taper that has lots of interesting possibilities when used with the mini toggle. When the mini toggle is in the up position the mid pickup is on and when the main toggle switch is in the mid position, front and bridge are together, it's a kind of out of phase sound which is perfect for some of Akkerman's rhythm parts. When putting the mini toggle to the down position it puts all three humbuckers on, up position on mini toggle changes nothing. The lower volume control also blends the coils when turned slightly to give back the neck plus mid pickups. The lower bridge tone control is not connected to anything. The bridge pickup has great bite with the main toggle down and the mini toggle in the mid position and there is good balance across the strings. When the mini toggle is placed down the bridge and mid pickups are on. Again the mini toggle in the up position does nothing. There is an incredible variety of tones available here. The ceramic capacitor is connected to the bridge volume control and is difficult to see as there is a lot of wire going to it so I don't move this in case anything comes off it but is does look like a .022 value nonetheless which is a common cap used with humbuckers.One of the things that stand out for me is that there is very little drop in volume: it does not lose the character of these pickups and it has bags of tone. This guitar has undergone many changes over the years with Akkerman in continual pursuit of great tone: through experimentation he has, since late 2012 and for now settled with this combination of hardware.

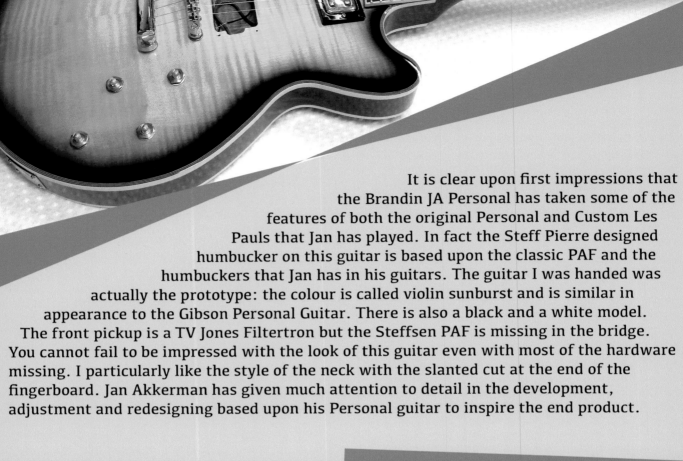

It is clear upon first impressions that the Brandin JA Personal has taken some of the features of both the original Personal and Custom Les Pauls that Jan has played. In fact the Steff Pierre designed humbucker on this guitar is based upon the classic PAF and the humbuckers that Jan has in his guitars. The guitar I was handed was actually the prototype: the colour is called violin sunburst and is similar in appearance to the Gibson Personal Guitar. There is also a black and a white model. The front pickup is a TV Jones Filtertron but the Steffsen PAF is missing in the bridge. You cannot fail to be impressed with the look of this guitar even with most of the hardware missing. I particularly like the style of the neck with the slanted cut at the end of the fingerboard. Jan Akkerman has given much attention to detail in the development, adjustment and redesigning based upon his Personal guitar to inspire the end product.

One of the Brandin prototypes in the factory and below, Jan playing a finished guitar.

Framus Jan Akkerman 1974,
First tribute model.

I take a measurement of 42.44mm/1⁴³⁄₆₄″ (the Gibson Personal is 42.43mm!), that's quite impressive for a manufacturing tolerance. Peter tells me that he works on the frets when the guitars arrive in Holland to give it a nice played in feel. This prototype hasn't had that treatment yet but they are still very well seated with no noticeable sharp edges. The other thing I do is to tap each fret and listen for a certain tone: this determines for me whether the tang of the fret wire has made contact with the wood: in this case they all have. The nut is a dark brown plastic but is of the kind that is very hard and good for tone, not all plastic is the same in density and some nuts have a small molding channel underneath which is even worse. This is a solid piece, hand cut with impeccably cut slots. I really like the way the back edge of the nut is slanted away from the take off point of the strings which gives great freedom of movement to the strings. The headstock is very sympathetic to the aesthetics of the guitar and I think sometimes a great looking guitar can be let down by an imbalanced design but not this one. It has a simple shape, not too wide with a distinctive arch on the top edge. Jan Akkerman's signature adorns the face of the headstock in gold script.

Tuners are gold plated Kluson MS33G types and area smooth in operation and, unlike the usual Grover; do not add any unnecessary weight. The headstock thickness is 16.55mm/²¹⁄₃₂″ and slightly thicker than the Gibson and the headstock pitch is 14.7 degrees. Giving more downward pressure over the nut. This was approximately what Gibson used on their headstocks until they started breaking because of the tension. They then changed to 17 degrees and supported it with a volute for added strength. Gibson original headstock pitch was 17 degrees but changed to 14 degrees from 1965 – 1973 and introduced a volute around 1970 for added strength but reverted to 17 degrees with some models later on.

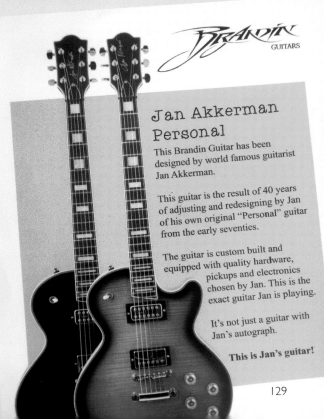

Jan Akkerman Personal

This Brandin Guitar has been designed by world famous guitarist Jan Akkerman.

This guitar is the result of 40 years of adjusting and redesigning by Jan of his own original "Personal" guitar from the early seventies.

The guitar is custom built and equipped with quality hardware, pickups and electronics chosen by Jan. This is the exact guitar Jan is playing.

It's not just a guitar with Jan's autograph.

This is Jan's guitar!

129

The neck is made from three pieces of mahogany with a Macassar ebony fingerboard with 22 medium jumbo frets measuring 3mm/⁷⁄₆₄" and the frets sit on the edge of the binding. Mother of Pearl bock inlays are very cleanly done with none of the usual filler around the edges. Macassar ebony is very smooth to the touch. The grain can vary from one board to the next as can the colour but the density will undoubtedly contribute to its resonance. It is similar in appearance to Rosewood and is very strong. At the 12th fret it measures 52mm/2³⁄₆₄", the exact same as the Gibson Personal.

The body is mahogany with sound chambers that also helps keep the weight down to a very manageable 8.14lbs (which will change slightly when some more hardware is added). The top of the guitar is finished in a beautiful Tiger stripe maple with excellent book-matching and is not a veneer. It is nice to see that the Brandin Akkerman guitars that are in the factory with this finish had consistent tops, no mismatching. The other thing I notice is that the lacquer is not overly thick as this could mute a lot of tone especially when using polyurethane finishes. The thickness of the body is 47.58mm/1⅞" and 43.2mm/1¹¹⁄₁₆" without binding and has a maximum width of 356mm/14¹⁄₆₄".

The bridge is made by Gotoh and now comes with Graph tech saddles (early ones were metal) and is adjustable by using two slotted posts that fit tight into the bridge which again is good for tone. The tailpiece is also high quality machined with only slight movement in the securing studs. The neck pickup is a TV Jones Classic and measures 4 ohms and is based on the 59' Filtertron version: it looks the part on this guitar. This idea obviously goes back to when Jan would've had a Gretsch pickup in this position on his black Gibson Custom around 1973. TV Jones is a US guitar pickup manufacturer based in Poulsbo, Washington and is known for manufacturing vintage style filtertrons. His pickups attempt to recreate the sound of vintage Gretsch guitars by using manufacturing materials that were used in the 50's and 60's by Gretsch. The company has been around since 1993 and was founded by guitarist and luthier Thomas V Jones in Whittier, California. The bridge pickup is called a Steffsen PAF and is based upon a Gibson late 50's humbucker: they are a perfect match for the TV Jones pickup at around 7.5ohms and hand wound. Four CTS volume and tone controls in this guitar date from 48th week of 2011 and 25th week of 2012. Orange drop capacitors link the front and rear pickups, Orange drop capacitors say SBE225P 10V 73k 1226 dating it 26th week of 2012. The routing is very clean and tidy and if the prototype is anything go by, the solder joints are substantial with quality wire.

As I walk over to the other side of the factory I take from the wall bracket a finished Jan Akkerman Brandin Guitar. I noticed the guitar diagrams on the wall for its construction dated 6/8/13. There have been various prototypes and tweaks along the way to achieve what we have here now. I plug back into the Kustom amp setting it for clean. The front TV Jones is very clear in reproducing each note played, it has amazing depth on the bass notes without being too muddy or losing articulation when strings are arpeggiated. Putting the toggle switch in the middle position brings in the Steffsen PAF which gives a kind of out of phase sound without being too thin. It has an almost electro-acoustic ring to it: the TV Jones pickup I'm sure is responsible for this. It is beautifully voiced with the bridge humbucker: I would use this combination more than any other twin-humbucker guitar because it does not sound too mushy as sometimes happens with high output humbuckers in the neck and bridge positions. The bridge pickup has a great attack, especially coming out of the mid-toggle position, some humbuckers in the bridge can be a little too hot which distorts even a clean setting on your amp and when overdriven can sometimes lose the character of your guitar altogether: this is not the case here. The strings just pick up very pleasing overtones without any of the nasties. If this guitar did not have Jan Akkerman's input in its design I would still regard it as a very high quality instrument that has great build and rewards you with long sustain in overdrive mode and is versatile for many styles of player. Akkerman has a unique and phenomenal expression and this is why he has chosen the hardware, pickups and electronics to reflect this experienced players' need for a wide ranging tone built guitar. This guitar comes with a Brandin Leather strap, extra strings, certificate of authenticity and the album "Minor Details" by Jan Akkerman. I would like to thank Jan Akkerman for allowing access to his Les Paul Personal guitar and special thanks also to Peter Herwegh, Pierre Van Wanrooij and Richard Keiser for access to the Brandin model and for their very kind help and hospitality.

Andy Scott 1963 Gibson ES 335

The Sweet was one of several glam rock bands of the early seventies: with thirteen top twenty hits to their credit. Blockbuster went to number 1 in 1973 followed up by three consecutive number 2 hits, Hellraiser, Ballroom Blitz and Teenage Rampage. The band definitely put the rock into glam and there are many superb clips which show just how well this band could really play. Shortly after the bands last hit 'Love is Like Oxygen' released in 1978, came the departure of the singer Brian Connolly. The guitar associated with Andy on so many of the bands early hits is a 1963 Gibson 335. For a while it was housed at the British Music Experience exhibition at London's O2 Arena, before being moved to Liverpool in the Cunard Building in March 2017.
I contacted Andy and he very kindly gave me his permission to get an in-depth peek at this fabulous looking guitar.

Before joining The Sweet, Andy's earlier group was called The Elastic Band and when he saw Ritchie Blackmore playing a Gibson 335 fitted with a Bigsby B5, he decided he had to get one for himself. He bought his Cherry Red 335 from a store in Manchester for the princely sum of £100 shortly before he joined The Sweet. At the time the guitar had a little battery powered treble booster fitted where there is a metal cap on the top of the lower cutaway. It gave a driven tone and made the guitar feedback too much so it was taken out. It was also reported that it was actually made from two guitars because of the two serial numbers found on it: one on the headstock and one on an orange oval label inside the 'F' hole on the bass side of the guitar. The story goes that this was due to fire that had broken out in the stores warehouse so they made one guitar from two damaged ones: but did they?

I managed to track down the Manager of Barratts Music shop, now retired and living on Anglesey, North Wales. His name is Brian Higham, and this is what he had to say. "The shop was called Barratts of Manchester – Percussion Centre and was owned by Fred Barratt. I worked there on and off from the late 50's to 1978" he said. He recalls "the fire was around 1967-8 and started in the drum shop on the corner of Oxford Road Manchester, and the guitars were at least 100 yards away, separated by a pub called The Oxford but part of the same building". Brian tells me that no guitars were involved in the fire and one of the staff had to jump from the first floor window when the fire broke out. The fire was even reported in the local paper at the time. He also suggests that one of the staff may have mentioned the recent fire and pointing out the discrepancy of the two serial numbers would give a credible story before selling the guitar at the discounted price of £100. At the time (1967-68) according to Brian, second hand 335's would sell for anything between £100 and £125. So as we look into the detail, could the guitar reveal the truth?

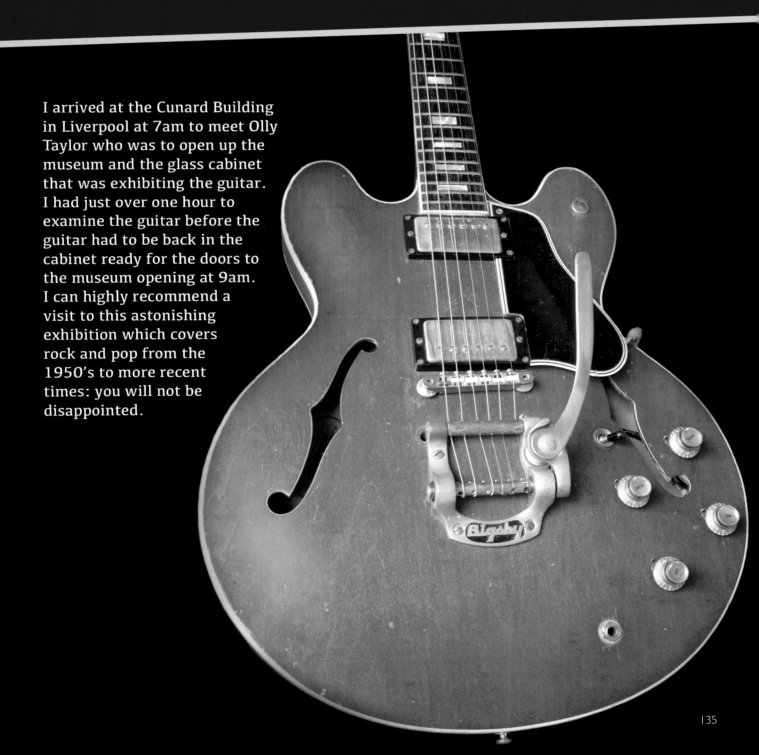

I arrived at the Cunard Building in Liverpool at 7am to meet Olly Taylor who was to open up the museum and the glass cabinet that was exhibiting the guitar. I had just over one hour to examine the guitar before the guitar had to be back in the cabinet ready for the doors to the museum opening at 9am. I can highly recommend a visit to this astonishing exhibition which covers rock and pop from the 1950's to more recent times: you will not be disappointed.

First introduced in 1958, the natural looking 335 had an unbound fingerboard with a dot inlay. Late 58 saw white binding added and a shorter pick guard was introduced by early 1961. Cherry red started to appear in 1960. Many retailers back in 1958 actually sold the 335 for $335:00. There were 804 Cherry Red 335's built in 1963 and a few of them still had what are called the 'Mickey Mouse ears'. It was about this time that they started to become less round as the jig wore out. This guitar still has the early appearance and the Cherry Red has faded a little: the laminated maple top has just a slight figure to it, visible through the translucent red. The overall condition is very good and obviously it's time in both the museums has helped to preserve this wonderful guitar from the rigors of touring. Although, in 1978 Andy spun around on stage in Australia and the headstock smashed into the drum riser and came off. Luthiers Maton, who still make fine guitars to this day, fixed it back on again. Looking inside the guitar the serial number 120808 is printed on the orange oval label and the serial number on the back of the headstock is stamped 121813. The reason for the discrepancy of numbers is that the orange label number denotes the year the making of the guitar started in the factory and the serial number impressed on the back of the headstock show when it was completed. The numbers on this guitar are not really that far apart compared to some which can be very different. It's not surprising that the guitar appears at first to have been made from two guitars as it wasn't until later years that the information about Gibsons' construction and their complicated number system became available. The other point about the headstock number is that it looks like a couple of the numbers have been written with a ballpoint pen, probably when the headstock had to be rubbed down following the break. The original stamp is still clearly impressed though. The respray on the neck is actually a much darker cherry than the rest of the guitar and the lacquer is quite thick, especially at the heel where it joins the body.

Around 1973 there was, just above the 'S' on the Gibson logo a small white gash on the black lacquer which is no longer visible possibly corrected by a touch up during the Maton repair.

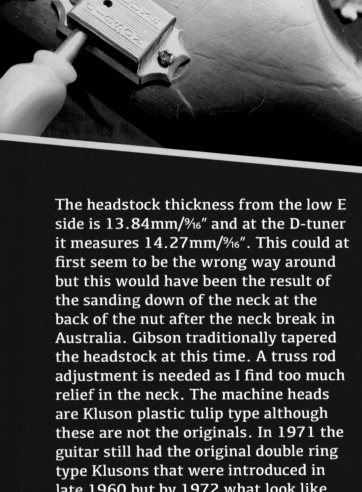

Replacement tuners

The headstock thickness from the low E side is 13.84mm/⁹⁄₁₆″ and at the D-tuner it measures 14.27mm/⁹⁄₁₆″. This could at first seem to be the wrong way around but this would have been the result of the sanding down of the neck at the back of the nut after the neck break in Australia. Gibson traditionally tapered the headstock at this time. A truss rod adjustment is needed as I find too much relief in the neck. The machine heads are Kluson plastic tulip type although these are not the originals. In 1971 the guitar still had the original double ring type Klusons that were introduced in late 1960 but by 1972 what look like metal button Schaller's' were fitted. The low E tuner casing on the back of this one today is coming away and is slipping, as is the D tuner but it's nice to see the look of its original state. The headstock has a 17 degree pitch, typical of Gibson's construction for the time. Sometime late 65' the headstock pitch was reduced from 17 degrees to 14 degrees to help reduce tension. It was later around 1969-70 they introduced the volute or 'bump' at the back of the nut to add strength to the area. Headstock width at the top is 76.61mm/3″.

137

The neck is made of Honduras mahogany and the difference in colour of the neck to the laminated maple body is a result of the neck being treated differently. Mahogany would need grain filler before the cherry lacquer is applied and will appear darker than the maple which in contrast is almost white close-grained wood. The neck is a touch darker than usual anyway due to the neck break and refinish. The pearl inlay block markers are neatly fixed with no noticeable shrinkage. The fingerboard is generally in good condition and the Brazilian rose-wood is smooth. Nonetheless I give it some oil as the fingerboard is somewhat dry. The Honduras mahogany neck is very slim and comfortable to play and you can see the Maton repair through the cherry lacquer. The bone nut has been replaced and measures 42.29mm/1¹¹⁄₁₆″ and the slots are much too deep on every string for maximum tone: also just a tad too wide. The first fret clearance though is just right but there is a gap at the end of the fingerboard before it meets the nut which shows shrinkage in the binding.

Frets measure 2.76mm/⅛″, are non original and much worn: every fret is flat reminiscent of the Les Paul Fretless Wonder. However Andy assures me that this helps him play the sliding positions up the neck as there is no high fret wire to restrict movement. Although these frets are wider, the binding has long since lost the nibs on the edge of the fingerboard. The action is very low and surprisingly there is no choking out. The first fret thickness is 19.55mm/¾″, the twelfth fret is 23.54mm/¹⁵⁄₁₆″ with the width at the twelfth fret being 52.09mm/2¹⁄₁₆″.

The thickness of the body is 44.81mm/1¾″ and feels really comfortable to hold. The centre block made of maple that runs through these guitars reduces feedback as the pickups, bridge and tailpiece (or as in this instance the Bigsby B5) are anchored. The Bigsby B5 fitted on this guitar is far superior to the B7: it just has a certain look that I like and is more stable in the tuning department.

There is a small hole with a wire coming out of it just in front of this unit that goes under the area originally intended for a stop tailpiece. And now this B5 covers it up: this would be for grounding purposes. Also a piece of the Bigsby unit on the treble side is missing, that should have a securing screw fitted as well. If you look just behind the Bigsby on the surface of the guitar there are tiny dots in the lacquer and it is slightly duller in bright light. This I am sure is a reaction to a sticker that Andy placed there about 1972 which stayed on for several years. The glue from the sticker has reacted with the lacquer here but thankfully it has not penetrated right through. Incidentally, the sticker was an anti-smiley face with 'shit' written underneath: the sticker was not spotted by the cameramen when the band appeared on Top of the Pops. The weight is 9.18lbs and is very nicely distributed, why have I never owned a 335: it is such a versatile guitar as we will see? The back of the guitar is in good condition with just two small patches of wear that look as though some touch up lacquer has been applied at some stage in the past. The other thing is that there are two small holes that look like strap buttons had once been there but I don't think they stayed long as there is no strap wear around the holes. The front of the guitar has lots of lacquer checking, especially around the 'F' holes but the general condition is good overall.

There were two types of reflector knobs that appeared around 1960 and up until around 1962: the first ones had a shallow post hole when viewed from the side. The 1962 reflectors knobs and later had a deeper post hole, meaning the post hole is much closer to the metal reflector cap. In this instance we find the later 1962 type. The upper section measures 17.61mm/¹¹⁄₁₆″ and the lower skirt is 26.10mm/1¹⁄₃₂″. The controls are Centralab but there was no time to take them out. When I plugged the guitar into a small Fender practice amp, there was no output, however, a few blasts of switch cleaner brought the pots back to life. The controls were very noisy and the jack socket was intermittent but some very fine wet and dry paper on the end of a screwdriver (smaller than a quarter inch jack) was put inside the jack socket. After twisting it around several times, it was just enough to clean off the build up of tarnish eliminating the bad contact. The treble tone control did not work until I moved a wire inside the 'F' hole to clear the short that was stopping it from working. These tone controls have a lovely smooth taper: at a guess they were probably Sprague Bumblebees.

Lifting out the neck pickup I take a reading of 8.34 ohms and there is a patent sticker missing from underneath: nothing alarming about that as sometimes they'd come off. The nickel plated pickup covers have not been taken off as the solder joints are very clean and there's no evidence of new solder. The other obvious clue to the story of one guitar made from two not being correct, is the neck joint at the end of the fingerboard is just how Gibson would have done the job originally. There is nothing to suggest any work, such as another neck being fitted, just the original one here. The routing is very clean and the red lacquer just under the pickup surrounds which are stamped M8 788 is slightly darker (not faded). The screws are also original. In late 1962-3 the 'patent' sticker was introduced when PAF's dried up. The bridge pickup gives a reading of 8.79 ohms and I carefully lift it out and the patent sticker is on the bottom of this humbucker. There is also a wire soldered to the pickup base which will ground everything electrically but is not a Gibson spec. This may have been done when the treble booster was fitted as higher output and sensitivity would increase noise, once again the cover looks to be original. The top of the cover though does show plenty of wear on the lower section. These patent sticker pickups remained like this until around 1966/7 when T-buckers appeared: they were called this because the moulding on the plastic bobbins had a 'T' embossed on them. Gibson made a mistake with the patent number they used which was 2.737.842 as this was Les Paul's trapeze tailpiece patent, but he didn't know about this until many years later. The patent number was used apparently as a smokescreen for pickup patent details in the 1960's. Patent numbers were then stamped on the bottom of the humbuckers metal plate from 1974.

Pictures of this guitar from the 1971 period show metal saddles an ABR-1 bridge with no retaining wire. The bridge today though has five nylon saddles and one metal one on the bottom E string and also a retaining wire. These would have appeared during late 1962: the notches are a little deep but spaced well. The threaded post's upon which the bridge sits is 72.88mm/2⅞″ wide point to point: the bridge is 84.57mm/3⁵⁄₁₆″ and is a tight fit.

Using the small Fender practice amp for testing, the bridge pickup is bright with lots of top end harmonics on a clean setting. Flick to overdrive and it is a Hellraiser: no muddiness, just a dynamic response to your playing style and a perfect riff sound. The middle position has the lovely openness you can only get with a semi, where both pickups work together and make you want to try all your jazz chords in a way you wouldn't bother on a strat. The neck pickup is a beautiful warm tone monster. When you back off the volume it tames the attack but leaves a lovely edginess that breaks up the clean setting on your amp to make for a really expressive sound. To get an idea of this watch Andy on Musikladen 1974 playing a track called 'Sweet FA' which not only demonstrates his ability and control over his B5 Bigsby, but the tonal variety that he achieves from this guitar. From the same show, the song Set Me Free is classic Queen with harmony guitars and brilliant harmony vocals before Queen ran with this format. The song Love Is Like Oxygen used this guitar and a tiny Vox Escort amp for the opening riff: in fact it is not until you compare the hit singles of Sweet with the rock band Sweet that you realise just how wide the tonal range of the 335 is when it is in capable hands.

The glam rock era could at first appear that it was more about the image than any ability to learn your craft and deliver the goods, not so with The Sweet who proved that behind all that glitter was a well rehearsed live band of accomplished musicians. Andy Scott's guitar skills using this Gibson 335 show a different side to the Hellraiser hit days and the versatility and competence of the player and this guitar is plain for all to see. Many thanks to Kevin McManus and Olly Taylor at the BME for their help and of course to Andy Scott for allowing access to this guitar.

"In 1968 I had seen Eric Clapton and Ritchie Blackmore playing 335s and loved the sound. I was using a Strat with my band pre-Sweet 'The Elastic Band' and knew I had to get my hands on a 335. I found my 1963 Gibson ES 335 TDC block inlay in Manchester and luckily it had a solid body short tail Bigsby fitted which allowed the tremolo arms to sit higher off the body providing great movement up and down. This guitar became my "Hit-maker" throughout the 1970s and after research by Steve Clarke I know more of the guitar's history than I did before. A truly historic guitar"

- Andy Scott

Paul Kossoff Isle of Wight 1959 Les Paul 'Stripped Burst'

Anyone who is a Free/Paul Kossoff fan would no doubt recognise immediately this guitar. It has not been seen for many years and my personal enquiry goes back two years. The owner has very kindly agreed to let me have a look at this guitar in a level of detail never seen until now. After much discussion of the meeting place we finally settle on a neutral venue where I booked a small room at a photographic studio. Here I get access to good natural light through the large overhead glass. Readers of G&B will recall that we had a look at another of Paul Kossoff's Les Pauls back in August 2015 (vol 26 #11) belonging to Arthur Ramm. However, over the years there has been a lot of speculation about this Stripped Les Paul guitar and the colour it may have been, suggesting that it has at some stage been a gold top or a sunburst. There have also been assumptions about the manufacturing date ranging from 1958 – 1960 because the serial number is missing following a refinish. It is going to be a fascinating chronicle exploring and in some cases challenging these assumptions. I even put forward another view as to whether this guitar is actually the one that was played on the timeless hit 'All Right Now'.

'All Right Now' was recorded at Island Studios, London on March 8th 1970 and the sessions for the album 'Fire and Water' began in February/March from which a different version of the hit was produced. As I am led into the upstairs back room of the studio the owner arrived promptly with two guitar cases: one contained the guitar and the second was just the original battered case. To my amazement on arrival the owner opened the case containing the guitar and then left the room for a short while in order for me to become quietly acquainted with it: no distraction or chat! Only later did I recognise the value of this perfect moment, enjoying the thrill before getting serious about the examination and measuring. The earliest known photograph of Kossoff using this guitar live was taken at the Le Golf Drouot in Paris during shows on the 5th, 6th and 7th April 1969. In May 1969 it is also seen in pictures at Morgan Studios hooking into a Wah Wah pedal, likely recording the tracks 'I'll Be Creeping' or 'Sugar For Mr Morrison'.

Other notable references are the UK show BBC Top of the Pops (TOTP) in June 1970, where the band are playing the classic single 'All Right Now' and later on August 24th. The German show Beat Club and the famous Isle Of Wight festival on August 30th 1970, here the band give a lesson in blues based rock and the individual parts played by each member with Paul Rodgers stunning vocals, make for one really powerful set. At the time of the sessions for Fire and Water, Kossoff could have used either the stripped burst or the dark burst 1958 Les Paul, serial number 82453 that he acquired from Eric Clapton when Free supported Blind Faith. It was on that tour in the summer of 1969 that he exchanged his three pickup black Les Paul custom for Clapton's dark burst.

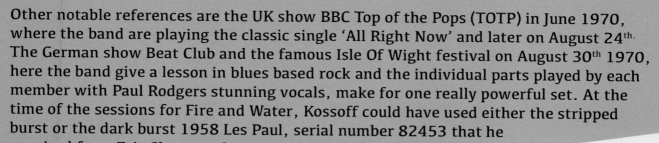

Due to the fact that Kossoff would use the natural fronted Les Paul for Top of the Pops, it is highly probable that a few months earlier this would be the guitar he was most familiar with for the actual recording: even though on TOTP, the band was miming except for Paul Rodgers doing an excellent live vocal. Kossoff appears to have an affinity with this guitar as evidenced by film and photographic footage of Beat Club and many live shows. How many guitarists Clapton, Page and others usually pick up and play the same guitar repeatedly because it served them well both live and in the studio despite having access to any guitar they want from a collection most dealers would drool over? Kossoff had small hands and although it is pure speculation, a large necked 58' standard might not have been his first choice of guitar to use for a long session. There is another telling point concerning the neck on the stripped Les Paul....more later.

ISLE OF WIGHT FESTIVAL
AUGUST 26-30 1970

FRIDAY 28th
CHICAGO
FAMILY
TASTE
PROCOL HARUM
JAMES TAYLOR
ARRIVAL
MELANIE
VOICES OF
EAST HARLEM
LIGHTHOUSE

WEEKEND £3

SATURDAY 29th
THE DOORS
THE WHO
TEN YEARS AFTER
JONI MITCHELL
SLY &
THE FAMILY STONE
CAT MOTHER
TINY TIM   FREE
JOHN SEBASTIAN
EMERSON,
LAKE & PALMER
MUNGO JERRY
SPIRIT   MILES DAVIS

SUNDAY 30th
JIMI HENDRIX
EXPERIENCE
JOAN BAEZ
DONOVAN
& OPEN ROAD
LEONARD COHEN
& THE ARMY
RICHIE HAVENS
MOODY BLUES
PENTANGLE
GOOD NEWS
RALPH McTELL
SPECIAL GUESTS
JETHRO TULL

DESIGN by DAVE ROE

PRINTED IN ENGLAND by ANVIL PRESS LIMITED

A brief history.

It is well documented that in 1974 Paul Kossoff's drug problem had got out of control and at this time he sold a number of guitars and one of them found its way to Orange Music, London: that guitar was the stripped Les Paul. It was sold to Mike Gooch for £500 on 21st Sept 1974. The frets at this time were badly worn and Gooch's father gave him an ear bashing for spending so much money on a beat up guitar. It was then refretted and also refinished on the front of the guitar but not the back. The original nickel plated pickup covers and stop bar tailpiece were replaced with gold plated hardware. Although the front had been refinished, the back was probably only lightly sanded down as the serial number was lost. The back of all Les Pauls from this period were Cherry Red. The work was carried out by luthier Dick Knight in 1975. When Kossoff's new band 'Back Street Crawler' played the Fairfield Halls, Croydon on June 15th 1975 Gooch took the guitar backstage to show Kossoff, Gooch recalled "as soon as he saw it, his eyes lit up". Kossoff offered Gooch £1000 and a Gibson L5S in exchange but Gooch didn't want to sell it. Some years passed during which time the guitar was almost stolen during a break-in but another guitar that was lying on top of the stripped burst case was taken instead leaving this treasure behind!

Gooch then decided the guitar would go up for sale but was unsold at Sotheby's London in 1993 and was later sold at Christie's London in May 1994 for £12,000. At the point of sale the guitar still had the replacement chrome tune-o-matic bridge with retaining wire and nylon saddles. Inside the guitar case was a worn ABR-1 bridge, gold plated in parts matching the pickup covers and tailpiece. It was believed that the bridge was the same bridge that had bowed under Kossoff's heavy gauge strings. The bridge was subsequently straightened out in a vice and refitted to the look of earlier photos. If you look at the guitar during Free's appearance on TOTP the saddles are metal although some say nylon and the top E saddle seems to have been flipped, as does the bottom E saddle too.

The look of the guitar today with its natural finish and highly flamed top is just breathtaking to see up close. The front of the guitar is in very good condition even though the refinish was done many years ago and the guitar has been played during this time. The back of the guitar though is a different matter and has remained original since Kossoff used it: the wear is substantial. Close up it looks like a map of an alien landscape with large sections of mahogany showing through without lacquer. There are dents, scratches and various degrees of fade: beautiful to my eyes anyway! As I place the guitar onto a table I take a weight measurement of 8.74lbs.

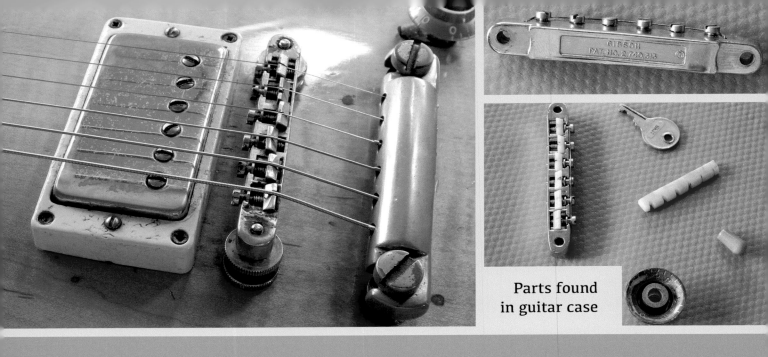

Parts found in guitar case

The bridge ABR-1 is measuring 83.90mm/3⁵⁄₁₆″ in length and 10.76mm/⁷⁄₁₆″ width. The B string saddle has been replaced and there is another cut in the saddle that is in the wrong place and the screw is slightly bevelled at the back. The top E saddle has not worn like the rest which suggests this was a replacement. Measurement from threaded post to post is 75mm/2¹⁵⁄₁₆″. It is worth noting here that this is the condition it was in when Mike Gooch purchased it so Kossoff in all probability could have used it like this. The slotted screw head is thinner suggesting it came off a non-original '59 ABR1. If you broke a string these were easily lost! The bridge is now almost completely without gold plating and what little remains can just be seen between the saddles and the lower part of the bridge. The fit on both threaded posts is tight and underneath the thumbwheels there is another set screwed down to the top of the guitar: again, this can be seen in some of the archive pictures. The spare bridge with retaining wire and nylon saddles came after 1962 and the one spare in the case is in fine condition. It's been said that Kossoff liked the mellowness of the nylon saddles: the tone was different than the nickel plated brass ones currently fitted.

The tailpiece is made from aluminium and the gold plating has almost disappeared and measures 101.72mm/4″. It is anchored down by two worn steel studs which are a very tight fit allowing more transfer of tone. The tailpiece is raised just slightly off the body and the strings just clear the bridge at the top back edge. Experimenting with the tailpiece by screwing it down flush to the body can give increased volume and tone but will raise the stiffness slightly. Lifting the tailpiece up can take some of the bass from the mix and many Les Paul players prefer the harmonics produced this way. A good compromise is the 'Joe Bonamassa wrap over' which gives the best of both worlds and Gibson for a short while actually did this on their guitars.

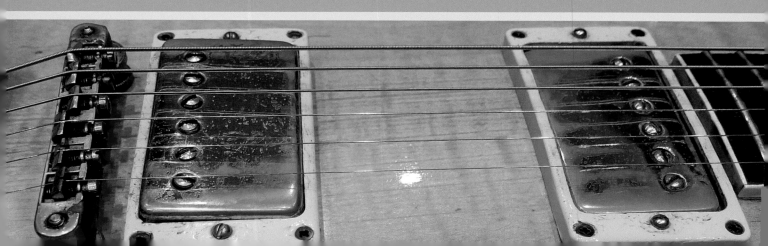

Incredibly these are the original bonnet style knobs and just as I spot that the rhythm volume control has been replaced, the owner produced the original! Apparently it keeps coming off but it is in fine condition. There is a lovely green tinge appearing around the bottom of the numbers so I take a picture of this original control before it is put away for safe keeping. The control pointers are still in place also which is nice to see. The control knobs measure across the mid section 18.72mm/¾" and the lower wider numbered part is 26.27mm/1¹⁄₃₂".

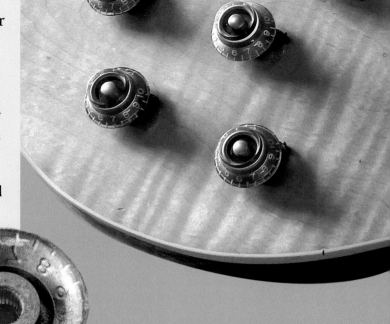

Original volume pot

The toggle surround or 'poker chip' as it is sometimes known is also original and has faded but you can, on closer inspection still see the lettering 'rhythm and treble'. In 1959, the lettering started to become more refined in size, the letter 'R' is slightly wider font than the 58's and the size of the lettering although very small is detectable. The 59's also started to appear with a thinner plastic, like the one here and this surround measures 33.34mm/1⁵⁄₁₆". The toggle switch cap has been replaced but once again, the original one is in the case! I take the plate of the back toggle switch and I can see that it has not been de-soldered which gives me a clue as to how the refinish cold have been done. The Switchcraft works perfectly.

Looking at the neck pickup first, which now has a very worn gold plated cover, the low E string pole piece reveals just below it a white bobbin. The owner tells me it is a double white PAF pickup so no need to worry about what that might have been. The pole pieces have no gold plating on them as originally they would have been nickel plated covers before the refit. Due to the amount of wear it looks really nice and has a DC resistance of 8.38 ohms. The bridge pickup is similar in wear and under the pole piece reveals a black bobbin. I am told it could be either a double black or zebra PAF and measures 7.99 ohms. From my experience, many double white PAF's appear to be slightly higher in resistance than other combinations but this in no way is consistent as many original Les Paul owners will testify. There is a point in mentioning that during 1959; double white or zebra combinations were a common look, by mid 1960 black bobbins were reinstated. The story often stated is that when Gibson took delivery of the bobbins before winding them, the company supplying them ran out of the black colour pigment in early 1959. Gibson didn't mind though as the pickup covers would hide them. The white bobbin is nearly always on the non-adjustable side with just a few exceptions. My personal view on this is that they probably did this for cosmetic reasons: I can't help wonder if there was a production suggestion because having a 57' black Les Paul Custom or a Standard with Humbuckers with a glint of white showing around the pole pieces would not look as good as if it had the black coil showing on the adjustment side. A black one would not be as visible as a white one. I think the exceptions were absent minded mistakes on the production line, as I'm sure repeating these combinations all day by hand was somewhat tedious. The M6.9 cream surrounds look great on this guitar: they would have an MR-490 stamped underneath with a 7 for the bridge pickup. The neck was an MR-491 with an 8 stamped. The measurement of the surround is 89.31mm/3½" in length and 45.20mm/1¾" width. The neck surround near the G, B and E strings shows excessive wear which is the area where Kossoff would play his solos and the plastic is quite thin so no need to take it off and run the risk of cracks appearing when put back as we know what lies beneath. I never take the screws out of a vintage surround anyway unless I now that the guitar has been out of its case for a couple of hours at least as this allows the cold plastic time to adjust to room temperature (expensive surrounds!) The maple top on this guitar is really striking and is a quarter sawn/flat sawn pattern using either Eastern or Hardrock maple and when you walk around the guitar it looks like venetian blinds opening and closing. The movement in this wood is hypnotic. Behind the bridge and tailpiece the holes have been filled where a B7 Bigsby would have been fitted. The white jack socket plate has been replaced by a large oversized one with slotted screws, it appears to be handmade and around the jack socket nut there are fine cracks.

Taking a measurement on the low E side shows a thickness of 16.26mm/⅝"
tapering towards the top to 14.55mm/⁹⁄₁₆". This is typical of headstock
design on many Gibson guitars until the early 1960's when the
thickness at the headstock tapered. The idea behind this was
to give the headstock additional strength as it was very easy
to break. Circa 1970 a volute or bump started to appear on
the back of the nut area to give more strength in this weak
spot. The black lacquer on this headstock is original to when
Kossoff owned it: there are plenty of cracks and
general wear and tear and around the edge of the
headstock the holly veneer is showing through.

  Between the A string tuner and B string tuner
there is a small chip of missing lacquer which
appears in photos and film around the time of the
Beat Club shows.....ouch! The Grover machine heads
have a smooth operation but in the past the machine head string
posts seems to have had larger washers fitted as there are visible
impressions in the lacquer where they had been. Originally this
guitar had Kluson single ring tuners: during 1960, double ring
started to be phased in. Around 1974 the tuners were replaced
with Grover Rotomatics and would be gold plated. (This
would be before Mike Gooch bought it) Looking at the
back of the headstock there are offset screw holes
which indicate between the Klusons and the Grovers
there had temporarily been another set put on which
would explain the larger impressions in the headstock lacquer.
The headstock width across the top edge is 78.54mm/3³⁄₃₂".

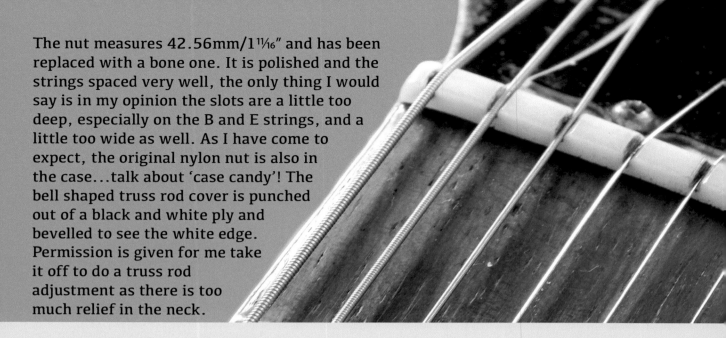

The nut measures 42.56mm/1¹¹⁄₁₆″ and has been replaced with a bone one. It is polished and the strings spaced very well, the only thing I would say is in my opinion the slots are a little too deep, especially on the B and E strings, and a little too wide as well. As I have come to expect, the original nylon nut is also in the case…talk about 'case candy'! The bell shaped truss rod cover is punched out of a black and white ply and bevelled to see the white edge. Permission is given for me take it off to do a truss rod adjustment as there is too much relief in the neck.

The fingerboard is made of Brazilian rosewood which is a harder wood than Indian. The condition is very good with no serious shrinkage on the crown inlays. On the second fret between the D and E strings there is just a little wear on the rosewood: it's remarkable that with such pedigree there isn't more wear here but I suspect this is due to the way Kossoff played. Kossoff had a very fast vibrato so unlike other players who would vibrate the string from side to side or possibly have long fingernails that would eventually leave behind some wear, he often would bend the note and then use his fast vibrato. This inevitably had some impact upon the fret wear. Having said that, it is not surprising that it needed a re-fret when Mike Gooch bought it. The frets were changed again in 2009. They are very well done with nicely rounded fret ends: frets measure 2.61mm/⅛″. The other thing to mentions is that the frets were cut individually so as not to lose too much of the nibs on the fingerboard binding. You can still see where they were. The binding is original and the only thing I can see is that when the fret ends were dressed and polished, some lacquer would naturally be lost so the binding has been masked off from the neck in the process and had some touch up lacquer applied which is very well done. Before Kossoff got this guitar it was originally a sunburst and there are still signs of red lacquer in the control cavity and the toggle switch area. The lacquer on the back of the neck and body is very road worn as you would expect from the period of time Kossoff used it. The heel is quite large but there is nothing unusual about that as you can find medium to large over the 59' period. Measurement at the first fret has a thickness of just over 20mm/¾″ and at the 12ᵗʰ fret 22.25mm/⅞″. The fact that is has not had a neck break is truly remarkable: Les Paul necks from late 59 into the sixties did start to gradually get slimmer. So although this is a slim neck it is not unusual. So, was the neck shaved as has been suggested? A measurement taken from the toggle switch area for thickness of the body is 49.41mm/1¹⁵⁄₁₆″ and in the middle at the back of the tailpiece above the strap button is 47.09mm/1⅞″. Fingerboard measurement at the 16ᵗʰ fret is 54.68mm/2³⁄₁₆″ which is consistent for 59' to 60' Les Pauls. It was common at this time for the backs of Les Pauls to vary in colour from deep cherry to dark brown like this one. Unlike maple, mahogany over time suffers more in oxidation and shade differences. This is partly due to the various shades of the wood itself and ultra violet light and absorption of this wavelength breaks down the pigment colour. If you have ever noticed how dark coloured objects feel warmer when sunlight shines on it, this is why. This is also why the red on the front of Les Pauls faded until early 1960 when the pigment was corrected.

When this Kossoff original sunburst was stripped, the back of the guitar may have had an overspray whilst the work was done to give cosmetic uniformity, as I can see no evidence of a complete refinish. This would of course lead to a loss of the serial number after a light sanding prior to overspray. The strap button is the same as the one seen in the Isle of Wight film footage and you can also see the unfilled holes where the Bigsby would have been at the edge of the guitar. The neck joint area has lost almost all of the lacquer and you can see the dark brown mahogany grain and joint showing through. So when was the guitar stripped of its finish and why? Of course we will never really know but it was indeed a common sight in the mid to late sixties to see guitars personalised. In fact, the folk singer Donovan reportedly convinced The Beatles that sanding down to remove the heavy finish on their guitars would make them sound better. Soon after at the sessions for the White album both Lennon and Harrison sanded their Epiphone Casinos. Harrison said "once they removed the finish they became much better guitars". This was in 1968, so could it be that this thinking inspired the original owner to do similar?

Lifting the plate off reveals some interesting things: the owner preferred that I leave the controls untouched so photographing the pot code proved difficult as the numbers are stamped upside down and are on the side of the cans! Cameras don't like lots of obstacles like wires and capacitors in the way as it confuses the focus. I took some shots then transferred to computer the images: there was lots of grime covering the numbers but after putting the picture through various filters and adjusting contrast levels, bingo, I have a number which is 134839. This means these Centralabs pots are all original and from September 1958. This of course does not mean that the guitar was actually built then; many factors are needed to date a guitar like this. Due to the fact that Gibson would buy lots of components ahead of production it is quite common to see 1958 potentiometers on 59' Les Pauls or other Gibson guitars. The other numbers alongside the control are BA811 1053 which is a Gibson part number. I can also see 500k. C2 resistance value stamped. The C2 denotes the percentage of audio taper as per Centralabs percentage chart. Sprague black beauty capacitors are fitted which are known as the 'paper in oil' type. The pots have obviously been taken out for the refinish but I think the toggle switch wiring was just pulled through the guitar after de-soldering on the volume pots: no need to take the wire off the switch. When everything was put back after the refinish, the ground wire connecting all the controls (which would have been plain wire) was replaced with orange insulating wire. The ground wire from inside the body coming out of a small hole was soldered back on. I don't know why one of the orange wires is soldered to the braided wire when it should be on the back of the can, but it works just the same. The soldering won't win any prizes in a beauty contest but nonetheless everything is secure.

Plugging in this guitar through the Marshall Valvestate 8080V that I took with me was a must to achieve anything close to the historical sound and character. On a clean setting on the bridge pickup every string is clear with loads of harmonics coming forth as the chord dies away, the balance is superb with the bass string never fighting to be dominant. A set of 10's strings are fitted. Every chord up the neck produces a lively acoustic quality rarely found on later Les Pauls, especially those made during the 70's. Mid position gives a well balanced sound between both pickups, a really nice mid range sound with great depth, perfect for arpeggios or big chords. It has a kind of big Gibson 350T sound to it. The rhythm pickup does not make me cringe when selected, from the D string playing a chord or picking the notes it rewards you with thick warm overtones and none of that bass boom taking over the show (think Free – Oh I Wept and you've got it).

The tone controls have a lovely smooth roll off rather than shut off, typical of these capacitors. Moving over to distortion settings, or more like crunch, I try to dial in a close approximation of that sound that is in my view probably the best classic guitar sound anyone would want. I was reluctant to even attempt any Kossoff licks on this guitar but talking with the owner about the way Kossoff would play the opening A chord for All Right Now, I went for it! There are so many YouTube clips of people offering fabulous versions of it and although Kossoff played it differently rhythmically live than the recorded version, I settle on the TOTP version. Here you can see Paul lift his first finger on the second fret from the A to open G on the riff. As soon as I hit that chord THAT way, you just know that the character and balance coming from the bridge pickup nails it.

Little Bit Of Love

Words and Music by Paul Rodgers, Andy Fraser, Paul Kossoff and Simon Kirke

Recorded on Island by Free

155

Any riff you could choose to play from the Free catalogue will put you in that ball park immediately, just for comparison I did an A & B reference with a Les Paul Deluxe from circa 70-71, which was originally a gold top but had Humbuckers fitted around the time purchased. Another handy reference is the Deluxe top had been stripped and left natural just like the Kossoff one. Taking into account that the pickups on the Deluxe were T-buckers, the construction is similar and it also has Sprague caps fitted. The sound difference is remarkable in the fact the bridge pickup on the test guitar sounds harsh and brittle and lacks colour. By the time I compare the rhythm pickup we both cringed at the volume increase and overwhelming bottom end that takes away the finesse that the Kossoff guitar has in abundance.

The sustain from this guitar is awesome. I have said before that once a guitar has had the lacquer removed and reapplied in thin coats, it just sings. This is especially true of polyester and polyurethane finishes that can kill tone on guitars when applied too thickly. Another thing I think contributed to this guitars' lovely tone is that everything in the bridge and tailpiece area has great coupling which helps transfer the energy from the strings more effectively. Sustain is achieved by a combination of the right elements coming together to produce harmonic overtones coupled with classic PAF's. This is why cheap guitars made with inferior woods and components etc do not achieve this!

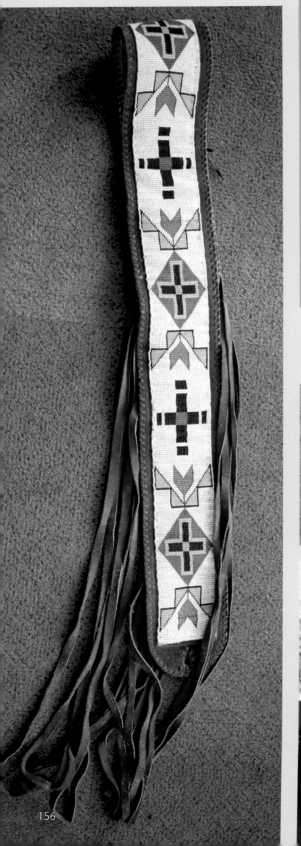

Guess who this case used to belong to...

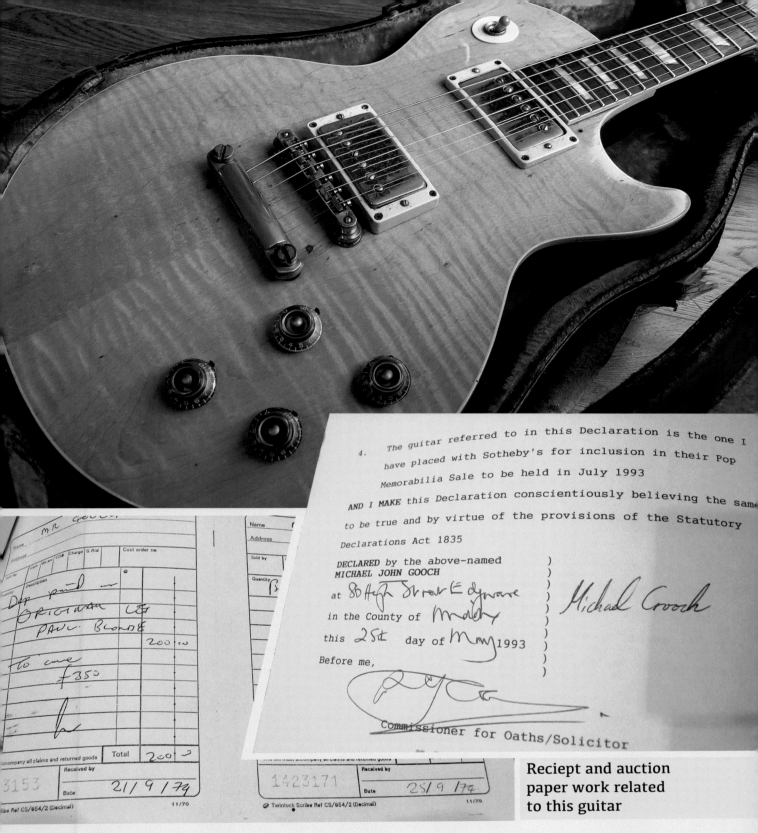

Reciept and auction
paper work related
to this guitar

It has without a doubt been a pleasure to look at this iconic guitar in detail, especially as I had like many had assumed that over the years it would have lost much of its original hardware, or worse, probably been re-sprayed and sold on, unrecognisable forever. The variety of tone from this guitar that produced the beautiful 'Don't Say You Love Me' to the solo on 'Remember' from the album Fire and Water is what Kossoff squeezed out of it. I have spoken throughout of details that when pieced together cannot lead to any other conclusion that this is a 1959 Les Paul Standard and I have a real feeling that this was indeed the 'All Right Now' Les Paul guitar. After all these years in the wilderness it is finally Free At Last!

Pete Townshend SG Special 1964

There is a letter from Pete Townshend explaining that he has no idea where or when he played this guitar but that it certainly is one that he used on the road in the UK, otherwise he says, it would not have made it into the cellar of his house that he lived in between 1967 and 1972. It was also possibly used on 'Live at Leeds' and Tommy recording, the letter affirms. A significant insight to the guitars background is gleaned from Pete saying that after spinning the guitars around and sometimes missing the 'catch', the delicate necks got broken and the bodies beaten up a bit. These bits he would take home to repair and at one point the letter states, he had three or four in various stages of repair. He would remove all the parts, pickups etc and use Cascamite glue which he found to be very strong. The letter goes on to say, one winter before the Thames barrier was built there was a flood and the basement of his house filled with muddy water. The guitar bodies survived but the pickups and other parts were ruined, some featured in a suitcase of old parts in the ICA WHO exhibition in August 1978. A few years on he bought with his wife a new house further down the river and while he was away on tour she sold the old house to her brother Jon Astley. Pete says in the letter "I forgot about the guitar bodies in the basement and Jon gave one to his friend and this is the guitar in question". He added that "although all the parts have been replaced he feels sure his neck repair will last longer than he will!" Having taken photos of this guitar and examined it in detail, as time was short the pickguard remained on the guitar. So initially this would cast some doubt on the age of the guitar but as you will read, deeper analysis will give a bit more credence to my suggestion as to the age. I have tried to find a timeline as to where and when Pete Townshend will have used the guitar and referred to video clips, still photos and even references from his book 'Pete Townshend – Who I Am'. These references provide some interesting contradictions to the official story and the letter but they are interesting in a way that makes the guitar even more fascinating and exciting to review.

November, 2014

To Whom It May Concern,

Gibson SRL No. 188776 (Year of Manfufacture : 1964)

During the late '60s I lived in a house by the river Thames opposite Eel Pie Island. This was in the period from 1967-1972 when I was still mainly using Gibson SGs on stage.

I did smash far fewer than most people think – but the necks were delicate, and sometimes I spun them around in the air and missed the catch, and the necks got broken and the bodies got beaten up a bit. These I would take home to repair. At one point I had three or four in various stages of repair. I would remove all the parts, pickups etc. and use Cascamite carpenter's glue, which I found very strong.

One winter, probably 1977 before the use of the Thames Barrier, there was a flood and the basement of the house was filled with muddy water. The guitar bodies survived, but the pickups and other parts were ruined, and featured in a suitcase full of old crap in the ICA Who exhibition in August 1978.

A few years on my wife and I bought a new house further down the river, and while I was away on tour she sold our old house to her brother Jon Astley. I forgot about the guitar bodies in the basement, and Jon gave one to his friend Andy ███████.

This is the guitar in question here. I have no idea where or when I played it, but it is certainly one I used on the road in the UK otherwise it would not have made it into the cellar in my house - so possibly on Live At Leeds and the Tommy recordings. Andy has added the correct replacement parts, and I feel sure that my neck repair will last longer than I will.

Yours faithfully,

PETE TOWNSHEND

161

The nut is just over 39.69mm/1⁹⁄₁₆″ and made of nylon. It is nicely cut and all the strings sit perfectly in their slots. Just at the back of the nut is a line of Cascamite glue running along it: I wouldn't want to change this nut as it'd probably take the headstock with it if you had to remove it the conventional way!

What I have found is my opinion based upon the photographs etc and also the story Pete gave in the letter. But a guitar with a 1964 serial number and a large pickguard (batwing) that strictly speaking should not appear till late 1965 looks puzzling until you break it down: not literally as is Pete's usual approach! I think this guitar body is the one famously used on the 1968 Rolling Stones Rock and Roll Circus film, evidenced by the distinct dark grain running across the top of the guitar: sure it has faded after 46 years but it is still visible. The large pickguard on the Rock and Roll Circus guitar seen in videos and stills has no pickup adjustment screws, only the holes where they should be. The pickups were secured to the plastic pickguard for easy assembly. This fact is another indication that originally the guitar had a small pickguard on it pre 1965 and the pickups were just screwed into the body. If you look at what Pete did on many of his guitars they rarely look original and some had screw holes visible where there would have been a Maestro Vibrola fitted. The other significant point to make is that this guitar has a large Batwing pickguard fitted that shows the holes as it would have been in 1968, but even without removing the pickguard I could see Cherry coloured wood through all of the holes.

Honduras mahogany body and neck: the bodies of these guitars were slab sawn, with the grain running parallel with the plane of the top. Necks were then quarter-sawn where the grain ran generally perpendicular to the plane of the fingerboard and the usual thin mahogany pieces were then glued to the headstock sides. In this case the sides have a huge chunk of Cascamite glue near the top edge instead of wood. The weight is just over 6.5lbs and the scale is 628.65mm/24¾". At the control cavity on the lower half of the body there is an extra piece from another guitar that has been glued on.

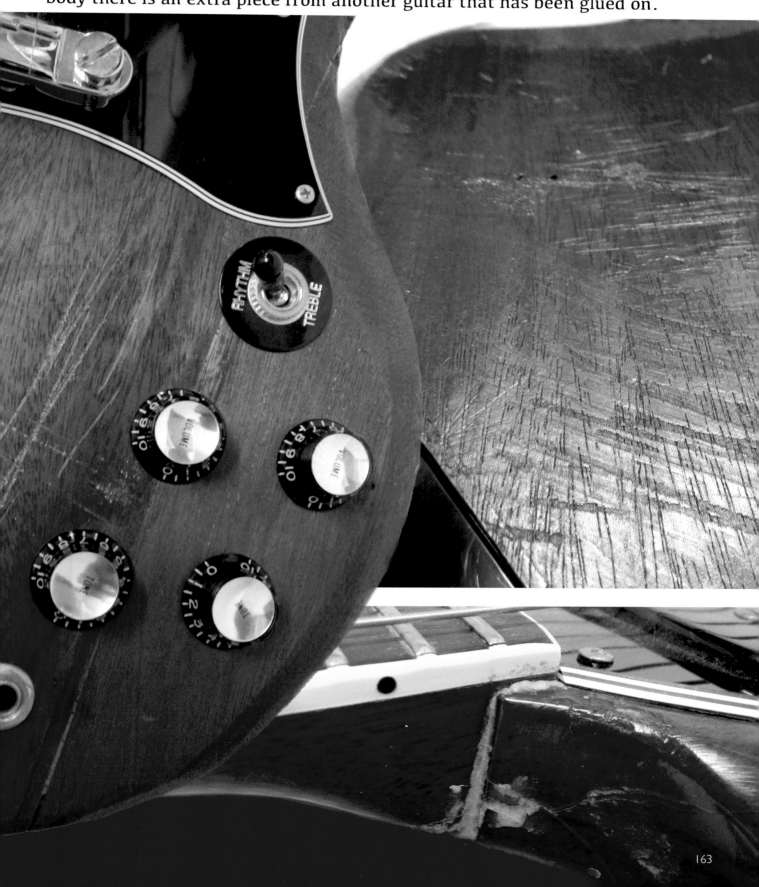

Between 14-16th September 1968, archive news footage and Pete's book confirm that there was a flood in the south of England: it was reportedly the worst flood to hit the Home Counties in the previous one hundred years: six weeks of rain fell in less than 48 hours. Three months after the flood, the Rolling Stones start filming for the Rock and Roll Circus which the Who appeared in on the 10th and 11th December. The guitar Pete is seen using in the film looks like a new SG Special with a large pickguard. It appears typical for a 68' but looking at still photos of this guitar I find it hard to believe that this guitar could have seen any sustained water damage and so could have been bought just prior to the filming. He did buy a reported 30 guitars from Manny's New York guitar shop in July 68 and he was recommended the SG Special. The guitar clearly has the wounds of a warrior that has been in battle: there are cuts, dents, scars everywhere, especially on the back which looks like it has had impact all over resulting in a huge piece coming off. A different piece has been put on from another guitar. Amazingly, the strike of my first chord reveals a vibrant, almost acoustic sounding guitar. It has a low action and good intonation. It is pointless to refer to the headstock pitch and whether it is 17 or 14 because this guitar has been so smashed up it could be between the two. The Cherry Red finish has obviously faded and the dark stripe I mentioned is fainter.

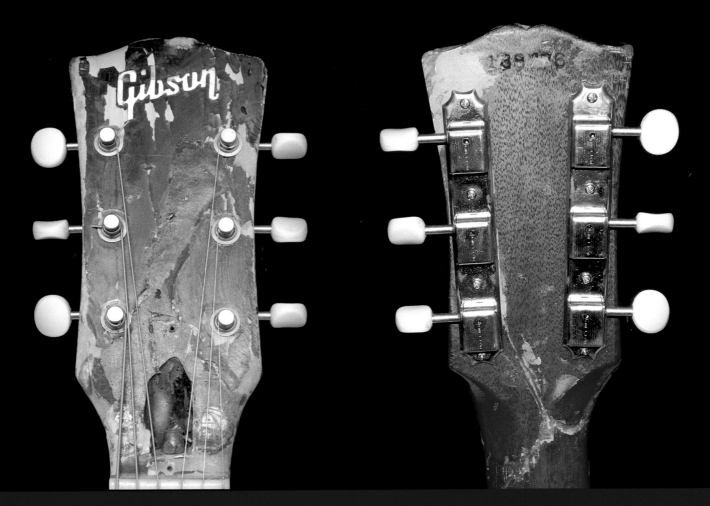

The holly veneer on the front of the headstock looks washed out and the mahogany on the top edge looks pale and dried out after it was damaged by water. Also, the black paint that has survived looks flakier rather than worn. Looking at the front of the guitar body and comparing it to the Rock and Roll Circus pictures, I am sure it is the same guitar body. All parts have been replaced by the current owner who is selling the guitar. Having analysed pictures and stories told about this guitar, I have come to only one possible conclusion that would explain these anomalies.

 Firstly, I think back in Sept 68' Pete already had broken guitar parts in his cellar, as he has said in his book that it was common for him to have three or four guitars in various stages of repair that he would bring home. I've seen photos of him playing a pre 1965 SG Special as late as 1971, with a small pickguard but there is also a very early photo of him playing one he borrowed from a support band in 66'. I suspect a neck from the cellar was then glued to the body of the Rock and Roll Circus guitar sometime later. There is Paris TV show film footage of him still using the Rock and Roll circus guitar on New Year's Eve 1968. It is very hard to find film or still photos of this guitar with its distinctive wood grain mark on the front body from 1969 onwards. The original neck on the Rock and Roll Circus Guitar was probably smashed beyond repair. The other thing worth looking at is the wood at the headstock where the black paint is missing, it looks very pale: almost driftwood in appearance and nothing like holly veneer, and what black paint remains looks flaky and has the appearance of water damage. This would certainly fit the story of guitar bodies and parts being in muddy water for some time as Pete suggests in his book. Lastly, some years on when his wife Karen sold the old house to her brother sometime in 1981, Pete said he forgot about the guitar bodies in the basement and Karen's brother Jon gave one to his friend.

So was it around this time that Pete put the guitar together? To me, the fact this guitar is made from three of Pete's guitars in no way diminishes its history. In fact it is a combination of guitars that he has used extensively from around August 1968 until 1971 and put together with newer parts giving it a voice once more. Although we could argue that it may not have the spirit of its original spec, it reminds us of the ghost in the machine that in essence was responsible for some of the greatest rock statements of all time. What is it about P90's that set them apart from anything else? These are classic sounding pickups and although these are not original to this guitar, the neck pickup is 7.74 ohms and the bridge pickup is 7.68 ohms. The volume and tone pots look like Japanese types: 500k that works perfectly with .02 caps and tidy wiring. The lower part control cavity that has been glued on looks like it has been routed at the back with small screw wood inserts that you'd not expect to see on an original SG Special.

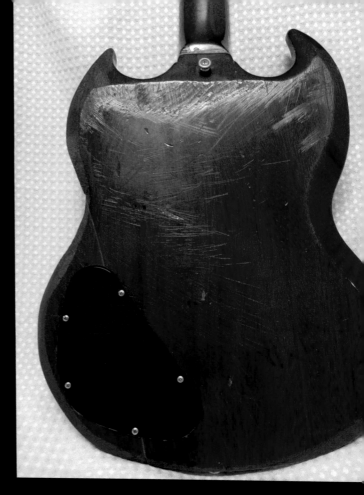

Not sure if Pete Townshend did this as he does not say so in the letter but is looks like it's been done with a professional tool. There is a faint line above this cut out where it originally should have been cut. The wood grain is not perpendicular to the rest of the grain on this guitar and another piece of wood has been fitted. You can see file marks and glue on both sides. Inside it has been painted with a black screening paint not original to this guitar but a good idea when starting afresh when re-wiring. The frets are medium oval original wire and still have the nibs at the edge of the binding, although they are nice and smooth with obvious wear but give the neck a played in feel with no sharp edges. If this is the early 60's neck it would make sense that this has seen a lot of playing because even in the tenth fret area it is worn.

Plugged into a Vox AC30 the bridge pickup is what you'd expect from these guitars: rich harmonic overtones with none of the top end associated with Humbuckers which is no bad thing as it gives a unique voice to this guitar. The middle position brings in a huge sound that when backed off with the volume control is almost electro acoustic and a great rhythm setting. Bringing in the neck pickup surprisingly doesn't shake the foundations but just reaffirms the beautifully balanced output with all the strings easily picked out when arpeggiated with the volume backed off just a tad. When full on with just a little bit of overdrive, these pickups sound so musical and expressive to any musical style you like. Listen to Pete Townshend playing the chords on See Me Feel Me: you will hear this expression cut through perfectly, reflecting the sentiment of that section of music. Then refer to Pinball Wizard Live at Leeds, does anything sound better than this. The SG Special is such a versatile guitar and sadly so overlooked today I wish I had it for a week.

Rock and Roll history exemplified in a guitar like this is a rare find. The fact that there are several parts on the body alone that make the whole, in no way diminishes its place in guitar history. It is still playable and the cosmetic appearance reminds us of the original owner's connection to this SG Special. It is still a living image of what

Suzi Quatro - 1969 Gibson Les Paul Bass Guitar

Suzi Quatro originated from Detroit and had a string of hits including 'Can the Can', '48 Crash' and 'Devil gate Drive'. She also played bass on the Cozy Powell hit record 'Dance With The Devil'. She was the first female bass player to become a major rock star and I remember her UK TV appearances with this huge Les Paul Bass. She moved it like the weight never mattered but it actually weighed 12.5lbs. Today she tells me that she has no problem with the weight, never has! This is a very rare bass to see these days and I can only associate Suzi using this to any lasting effect. The Les Paul bass stands out to command your attention and with its dark walnut finish still looks classy and like it means business. The Les Paul bass is often called the Les Paul Recording or the Les Paul Professional but these were the names of the six-string guitars: Gibson's own literature only ever describes this model as the Les Paul Bass. I asked Suzi where she bought it and she told me before she came to the UK she actually went to the Kalamazoo factory to get it. I explained what I was going to do to her guitar as regards opening it up and checking the inner workings and she reassuringly gave me the go-ahead. The first thing I do is take it over to a window to let natural light fall upon it. I carefully lay the guitar down and flip it over to reveal the control plate. This is going to be interesting!

  Wow, I don't think my house has this much wiring! Red, green, blue and brown wires are coming from the pickup cavities and distributed around the components: all very tidy. There is no movement in any of the wires when you turn the guitar from side to side, a factor I am sure in its design that the high grade stiff wire would not cause potential failures or dry joints in this busy assembly.

The solder joints are some of the biggest blobs of solder I have ever seen. As this is a low impedance guitar it needed a low impedance amp like the LP12 that was released at the same time. The LP12 is an LP1 pre-amp with an LP2 cabinet. Another way to plug in is to use an AD1 Low–High impedance transformer cord. Both the Les Paul Bass and later the Triumph Bass that appeared in 71' were recording bass's for the studio but were still a great live instrument. To date this bass, a number of factors are considered, firstly all three pot codes are 1376944 which takes us to 1969 in the 44th week (October), 137 being the manufacturer CTS (Chicago Telephone Service). This alone should not be used to date the guitar but used only as a back up and guide when the serial number is missing or a re-spray has taken place. However, knowing also the period of time that these bass guitars were actually produced, from late '69 to 71 at which point it was changed to a Les Paul Triumph, does give me the confidence that when added to the fact that Suzi went to the Kalamazoo factory to get it does narrow this down somewhat. It is fitted with a tiny Sprague capacitor and not the usual bigger striped ones seen in many Gibsons.

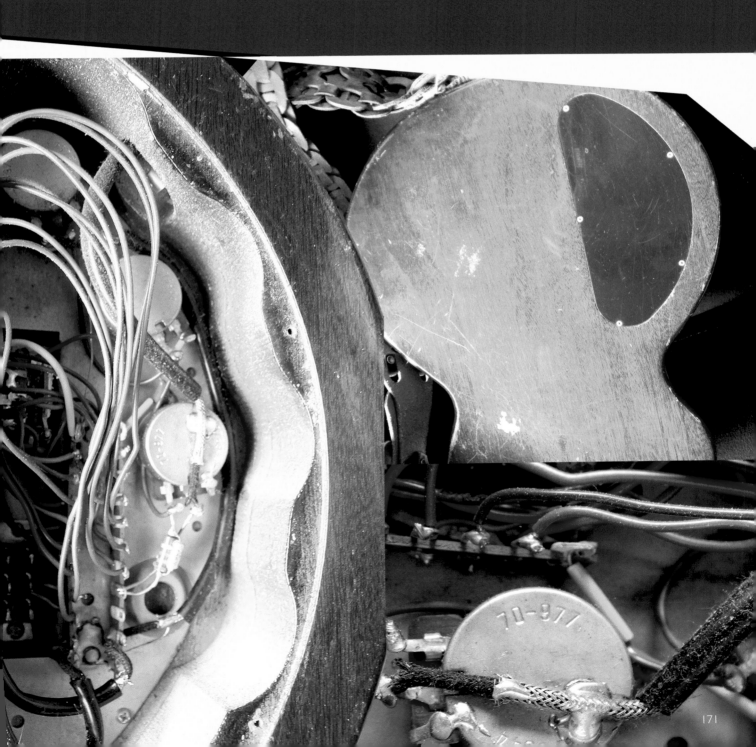

It was around 1967 that talks began with Gibson about Les Paul's idea of low impedance pickups. These pickups were revolutionary at the time due the fact they gave a very clean sound. The first guitar to use them was the Les Paul Personal: the slanted low impedance Humbuckers were designed for a broader string response. The guitar pickups used 24 gauge wire but the larger bass coils were of 32 gauge wire. There is approximately 160 feet of wire in each pickup and the coils were then sealed in a thick epoxy that kept everything in place. The pickup part number on the Les Paul bass and Triumph from 1969-71 is 13555 front and 13560 bridge. Typically on this model each pickup would have three different layers of pickup windings with control to select between them.

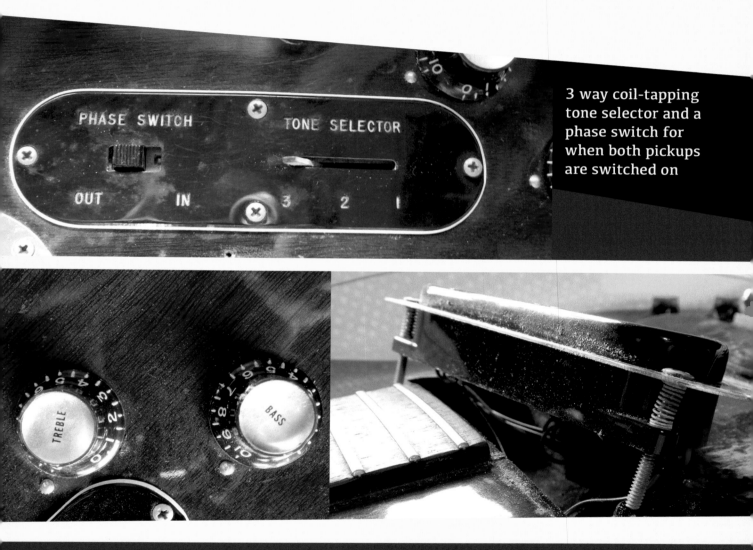

3 way coil-tapping tone selector and a phase switch for when both pickups are switched on

These have an impedance of just over 50 ohms. I took out the front pickup and I couldn't believe how heavy it is at just less than 1lb. I did not want to pull the pickup out completely as all the wires coming out of this pickup are under tension and I don't want to risk any potential fractures to this very busy pickup. The cavity is about one and a half inches deep and the routing is clean with no splinters anywhere. The pickup height can be adjusted by three screws and the black pickup cover has Gibson embossed on top and the pickups measure 34mm/1⅜" by 107mm/4¼". The tone switch on the guitar gives incredible variety: you wouldn't expect anything less from Les Paul though would you. Position one gives extra deep bass whilst position two gives normal bass frequencies of around 66.2k and position three will give a high pitch sound at 127.9k. The pickups are surrounded by an attractive chrome plate that sets the look off well. All the screws are larger than you would expect to see on any Gibson guitar.

A switchcraft toggle is sitting in a very tidy well cut cavity with no rough edges. You get a feeling with this guitar that attention to detail was priority in development. The selector switch is suspended with a thick rubber grommet type of surround as you'd expect to see on an ES175. Volume, treble, bass controls are marked with estacion pins. There is a three-way tone selector switch similar to one you'd see on a Fender Telecaster: this one has lost the plastic tip though. The switch connects to a coil tap wired circuit with phase switch on a small oval chrome plate. Also the bass control on this guitar actually adds a little volume when you turn it up but with the treble unaffected.

The nut is 38mm/1½" and looks to be original: it's well cut with no overhang at either end and is made from bone. The strings sit well in their slots although the E string could have gone a little deeper covering just half of the string.

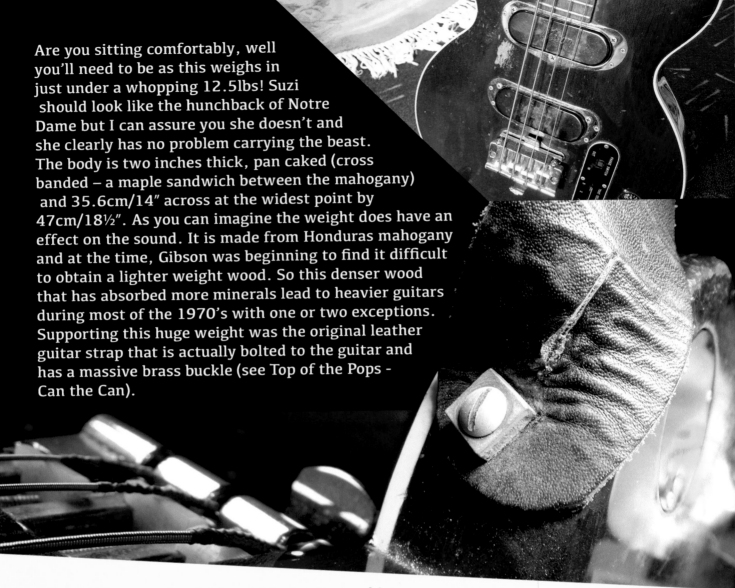

Are you sitting comfortably, well you'll need to be as this weighs in just under a whopping 12.5lbs! Suzi should look like the hunchback of Notre Dame but I can assure you she doesn't and she clearly has no problem carrying the beast. The body is two inches thick, pan caked (cross banded – a maple sandwich between the mahogany) and 35.6cm/14" across at the widest point by 47cm/18½". As you can imagine the weight does have an effect on the sound. It is made from Honduras mahogany and at the time, Gibson was beginning to find it difficult to obtain a lighter weight wood. So this denser wood that has absorbed more minerals lead to heavier guitars during most of the 1970's with one or two exceptions. Supporting this huge weight was the original leather guitar strap that is actually bolted to the guitar and has a massive brass buckle (see Top of the Pops - Can the Can).

The finish is not that bad considering its working history as the lacquer is still good with none of the usual checking cracks that you'd expect to see on a guitar of this vintage. Sure there are lots of dents and scratches and there is a noticeable wear patch between the front and rear pickups where Suzi would have rested her thumb. The back of the neck still has its lacquer intact. The neck is made of three-piece mahogany with the usual side pieces on the headstock that can clearly be seen. This was a standard method of build as it saved wood by not having to machine a wider piece of mahogany which would be costly and unnecessary. At the time this was built, Les Paul Deluxe's had a one piece neck but interestingly did not have the cross banded body until a little later even though this guitar has it! It becomes clear that Gibson had a blueprint of a model and started production on its guitars but like any manufacturer made slight changes for improvement along the way. Even their own catalogues could not be relied upon when looking at hardware or construction as a pre-production model very likely had differences and this bass is surely one of the very few built this way. This neck is Honduras mahogany with Brazilian rosewood fingerboard: I've noticed that rosewood tended to be more open-grained which is consistent with what you'd expect to see on the late 50s guitars. Later guitars with rosewood fingerboards had a more tight grained appearance, nothing wrong with that, it's just down to the age and origin of the wood. The fingerboard is in very good condition with no visible shrinkage or sunken grooves you may expect to see and the fret ends are nice and smooth. Abalone dots are well cut and feel smooth and flush to the fingerboard. I don't normally measure the fingerboard as a rule but I did on this one and will explain why.

The fingerboard measured 58.4cm/23" from just in front of the nut to the end of the neck and has 24 frets. The scale length is 77.5cm/30½" and joins the body at the 16th fret and measures 53mm/2²⁄₁₆" at this point. The fact that a lot of the board and neck goes into the body makes for a good coupling and string vibration connection giving huge stability and sustain. I asked Suzi if it will be ok to do a little TLC whilst I have my tools with me and she agreed. So as the fingerboard is very dry I oiled it with linseed oil and adjusted the truss rod as it was starting to back bow although the strings are not rattling because the action is quite high and the notes are clear. Having oiled the fingerboard twice it took on a luxurious dark chocolate look and seemed all the better for it. The truss rod though is a different matter as it was too loose to make any noticeable difference to the neck. I have a 73' Les Paul Custom with exactly the same problem. The only way to get some correction for this type of problem is to put a piece of wood with spacers underneath it near the 5th and 7th fret area, clamp it and heat it for about 45 minutes keeping an eye on the neck. When you remove the clamps you should have a slight dip in the fingerboard so the truss rod becomes tight again to allow some degree of adjustment. Don't try this at home though if you are unsure as you could damage the lacquer.

Anyway the problem is not that serious on this neck: I have seen much worse but it is worth keeping an eye on. Suzi did tell me that she's always had issues with this truss rod. The back of the headstock shows the number 860401 but because of Gibson's sometimes erratic numbering system. It can be a bit of a challenge to pinpoint an accurate date. But this number does date to around 1969 and added to the fact this was not a long production guitar, again, I'd say 1969 fits. Chrome plated Schaller M4 machine heads are original and work perfectly. I did tighten the screw on the D machine head slightly to adjust the torque. The Gibson Mother of Pearl logo is damaged between the letters B and S and I think the crown motif looks better on this dot fingerboard.

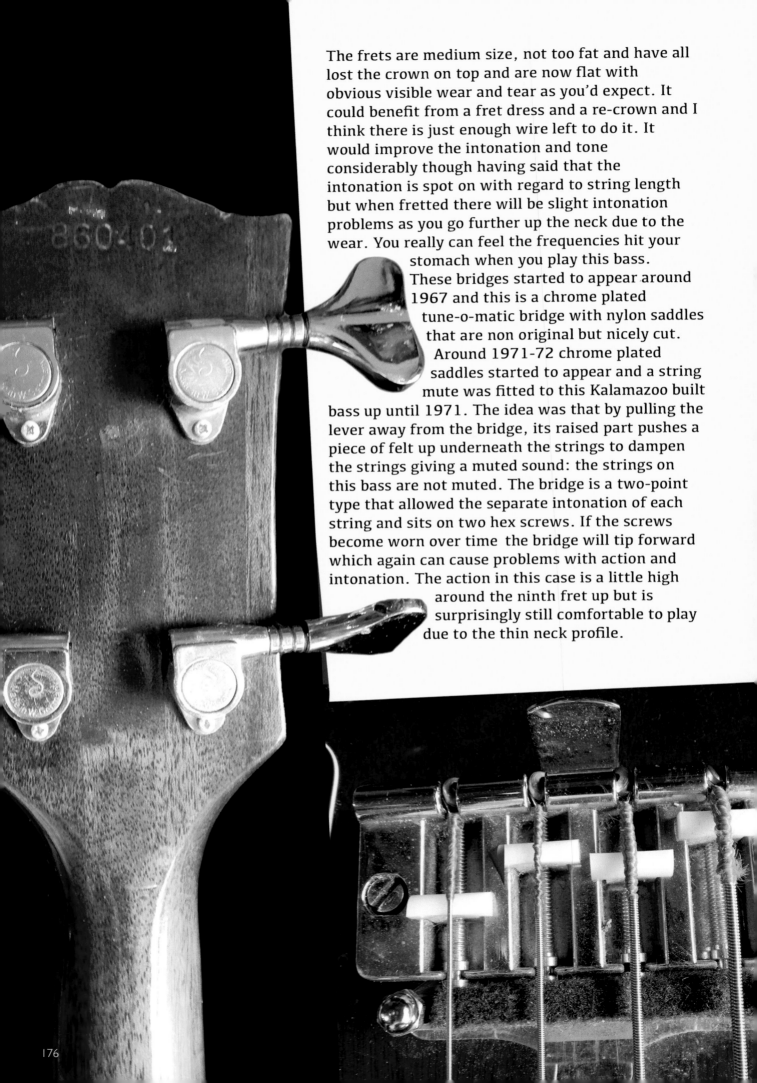

The frets are medium size, not too fat and have all lost the crown on top and are now flat with obvious visible wear and tear as you'd expect. It could benefit from a fret dress and a re-crown and I think there is just enough wire left to do it. It would improve the intonation and tone considerably though having said that the intonation is spot on with regard to string length but when fretted there will be slight intonation problems as you go further up the neck due to the wear. You really can feel the frequencies hit your stomach when you play this bass.

These bridges started to appear around 1967 and this is a chrome plated tune-o-matic bridge with nylon saddles that are non original but nicely cut. Around 1971-72 chrome plated saddles started to appear and a string mute was fitted to this Kalamazoo built bass up until 1971. The idea was that by pulling the lever away from the bridge, its raised part pushes a piece of felt up underneath the strings to dampen the strings giving a muted sound: the strings on this bass are not muted. The bridge is a two-point type that allowed the separate intonation of each string and sits on two hex screws. If the screws become worn over time the bridge will tip forward which again can cause problems with action and intonation. The action in this case is a little high around the ninth fret up but is surprisingly still comfortable to play due to the thin neck profile.

The original Les Paul bass did not sell well and in 1971 the model was redesigned and called the Les Paul Triumph. The Triumph had switching to change it from low to high impedance and was slightly thinner with a chest contour, but it was still a heavy bass. Both the Les Paul Bass and the Triumph are very rare today and it would be easy to dismiss what they had on offer as simply designed for a studio situation. However, with the right set up for live use the Les Paul bass will offer a thunderous sound with clarity and definition that Suzi Quatro has no problem delivering. In my view this bass was ahead of its time albeit for a limited market. But without the ground breaking ideas from Les Paul coupled with his inventiveness, the world of guitar could have been very dull indeed.

Dave Hill of SLADE custom guitar

Slade rose to prominence in the early 70's glam rock period and were never out of the UK charts with 17 consecutive top 20 hits, 6 #1 records. The British hit singles and albums name them as the most successful British group of the 1970's based upon sales of singles. Gene Simmons of Kiss cites Slade as a big influence. If you look at any YouTube songs of Slade in the early 70's on Top of the Pops chances are you will see Dave Hill using this guitar. Dave tells me that this guitar was used on every Slade hit regardless of others he may be seen using on promo videos and shows etc. He says "It is the Slade sound as soon as you plug it in to a small Fender amp".

I was given permission to examine it: reassuring for me as I fully appreciate the sentimental value alone of this guitar bought for Dave by his father in the late 60's. So Dave had this guitar before Slade had any hits. So as I reach for the guitar (in a new Gibson case that fits it perfectly) I was surprised at the weight as I lift it out to look at it. Considering the work this guitar has done and its history, the condition of this guitar is, generally speaking quite good. Of course there's been some damage along the way and some headstock repairs but this a unique looking guitar with great history and vibe. The story goes that before Slade had success, Dave's father took him to London to purchase this guitar for him for £220 in 1968. It was built by Sam Li (Lee) who had a workshop in Gerrard Place in the late 60's, and this was in the window of the Shaftesbury Avenue shop when he spotted it.

The avenue gave its name to its guitars and Shaftesbury was the UK importer for a range of guitars from 1968 – 1974. The distributor was Rose Morris who also had the concessions for Marshall Amplifiers and Rickenbacker Guitars which appeared in the latter part of 1968. There was a Rickenbacker 6-string, a 12-string and a bass guitar: all of them were modelled on the 330 style of guitar. Hardware and pickups were vaguely similar to the originals and were of good quality: at least the ones I've seen were. Interestingly, the original toggle switch on Dave Hills guitar was metal which is very much like the 330 Shaftesbury Rickenbacker. There was a story I heard some time ago that said Sam Li likely worked on Peter Green's Les Paul! Although he had a reputation as a good repair man and working as a set-up man for Selmer's, he could also refinish guitars. Sam's strong point however was not wiring and guitar electronics.

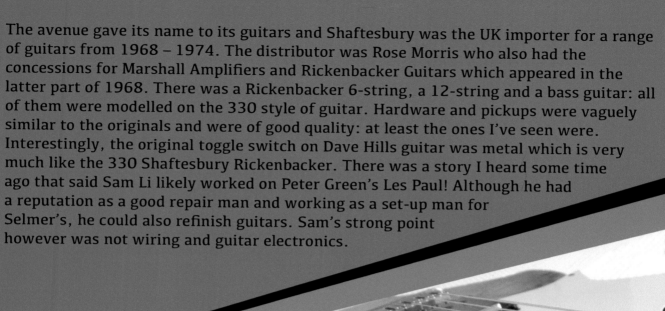

The first TV use of this guitar can be seen on a black and white film of Slade performing a Paul McCartney song called 'Martha My Dear' in May 1969. Having done a timeline on this guitar it is interesting to see when things got changed along the way. In January 1971, the track 'Get Down and Get With It' was released and the guitar at this point looks the same as when it was purchased, with a Humbucker in the bridge, a single coil in the neck and a large scratch plate surrounding both pickups. There was a separate control plate with two volume and two tone pots. The metal toggle switch is in the lower part near the bridge volume pot. A Gibson tune-o-matic bridge and tailpiece were fitted, then, behind the tailpiece was a small plastic plaque with the words Custom Made inscribed on it which is pinned onto the guitar. The plaque is slightly smaller than the Gibson 345 – 335 guitars as they would have small ornate squares at either end, original Gibson 345-335 guitars had the usual stop tailpiece to anchor the strings, but there were quite a few that were factory fitted with a vibrato tailpiece. On these guitars, the holes drilled on the body are either filled in with pearl dots or covered with a plastic plaque engraved with the words 'Custom Made'. But this guitar was not custom made for Dave

The large body of this double-cutaway guitar is made of maple, ochre in colour and worn away in the upper part where the arm would rest or in this case never be still! There is a nice shaped cut into the top of the body that steps down from the scratch plate, and another one on the far edge which tapers down and has discoloured over the years with wear: very smooth and shiny. From the large cutaways, the thickness is slightly more than a Les Paul Standard and the lower horn keeps the thickness along the bottom of the guitar as well but is bevelled.

There are plenty of the knocks and dents you'd expect to see and every one of them has a story to tell. The weight is 8.5 lbs.

The top horn is the same until the edge of the scratch plate where it starts to step down twice and gets thinner. There is another cut into the maple body which some would say is a bit over the top but actually looking at it from different angles I think it is tastefully done. The neck is a one-piece mahogany 345 Gibson that has been fitted very well. The headstock did have the crown inlay in the 70's but on the treble side where damage occurred the headstock repair has resulted in the whole of it being re-sprayed to all black and thus losing its crown. Not sure why the crown could not have been retained as there are ways to get around it but the repair is nicely done anyway. In the early days the back of the headstock was darker in the machine head area which tapered to just behind the nut but today it is all the same colour. The nut measures 41mm/1¹⁰⁄₁₆" and at the 12th fret 51mm/2".

The rosewood fingerboard is in good condition and the double parallelograms are nicely cut. A re-fret has taken place and the frets are thin and low with just a little wear making them flat on the top edge. Dave tells me later that the zero fret was fitted at the same time as the re-fret instead of the original bone one. There is some buzzing coming from the B string because the nut at the back of the fret has not been cut deeply enough so the string hits the top of the fret wire as there is not enough string pressure coming off it. The nut really is only a guide for the strings but it should be cut to allow the strings freedom when a zero fret is fitted. Intonation would need adjustments because of this zero fret when fitted. PP48 is stamped at the back of the headstock.

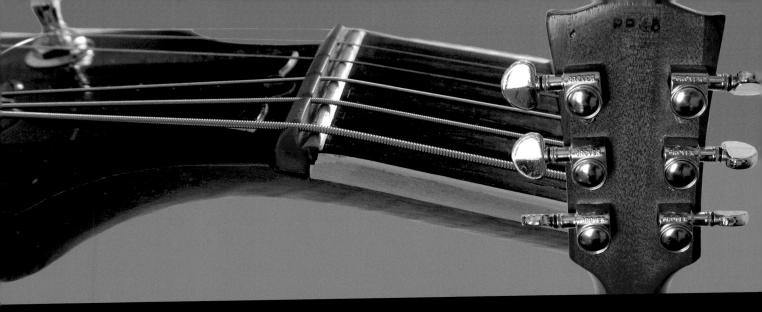

With permission, I do a little work on this and clean it up. The tang under the fret wire seems to be behind the edge of the fingerboard and glued with the nut which I don't think looks good or is accurate. A replacement to a bone nut would be perfect here to restore its original spec. The other point is a zero fret on open chords would make the sound brighter somewhat because of the metal instead of the bone.

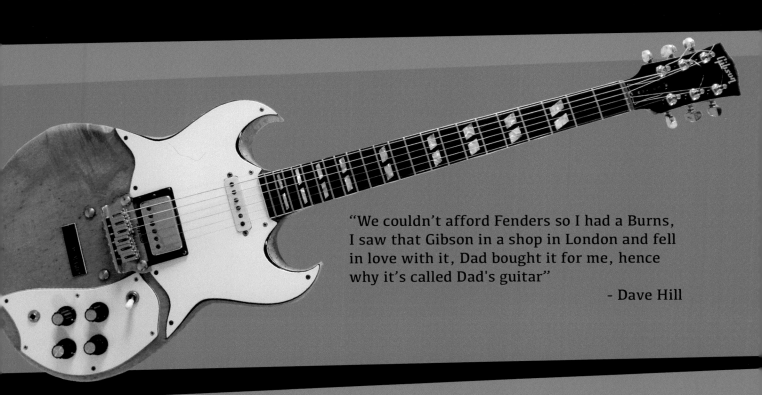

"We couldn't afford Fenders so I had a Burns, I saw that Gibson in a shop in London and fell in love with it, Dad bought it for me, hence why it's called Dad's guitar"

- Dave Hill

After oiling the fingerboard, this rosewood has a lovely dark chocolate look to it and feels much better. Truss rod adjustments are not needed as the clearance is just right although the action in my opinion is a little too low to achieve clear ringing notes. This could be due to the slight fret wear but a simple fret dress would sort this out. Grovers are fitted which feel smooth to turn: sometimes people over tighten these with the small screw at the end thinking that it helps to stop them from slipping, it doesn't. The screw is there to adjust the torque so that it feels comfortable to turn. This is such a comfortable neck to play and is quite thin at the back: probably mid 60's with great upper access and I can't help wondering what happened to the guitar it came off?

John Birch guitars started in Birmingham around 1970 and its founder members were John Birch, Arthur Baker and John Diggins who later went on to produce Jaydee Guitars. They had some very clever switching on their guitars for the time. John Birch would advertise the parts he made like pickups and offer customisation. In March 73' his new bridge design made of stainless steel which replaced the tune-o-matic bridge and tailpiece found its way onto this guitar and was first seen at Slade's Earls Court gig. This had brass pillar inserts to secure this very sturdy bridge with stainless steel caps to cover the top of the studs. Individual saddles with height adjustments and the steel plate they sit on which is about 3mm/⅛" of an inch thick delivers maximum transference of string energy. A 'John Birch' inscription is stamped into the steel plate. Just at the back of the bridge on both treble and bass sides is a number that looks like possibly T or C 258 which would make this one of the very early ones made. Judging from their condition, the saddles today seem to be recent ones. Also on the bass E string side of the bridge, the adjustment screw for intonation is slightly oval. At the back of the saddles secure springs hold them in place.

Over the years I have seen many suggestions about what these pickups could be so let's start with the neck pickup. It's a Fender Jaguar post 1965, not a Strat pickup as many have thought. The pole pieces are staggered and the two outer poles E and E are flush to the cover and the B and A poles are just below the rim of the cover with the D and G raised higher. The claw which is what you would see on the sides of the pickup has been removed. This metal claw was used to focus the magnetic field more, not to screen it. This probably is why people assumed it was a Strat pickup, also the top edges are squared like a Jaguar pickup. These pickups used 42AWG wire, insulation formvar, and the average number of turns was 8,550. Early Jaguar pickups measured around 6.26 ohms but this pickup on Dave's guitar measures 6.14 ohms. Moving on to the Humbucker, I don't take it out because the screws have gone completely rusty and although I have the tools with me to get them out, I tell Dave that I am leaving them in. If I'd have taken them out I would have to put replacements in which would require aging so they are sympathetic to the rest of the hardware. There is a hairline crack on the pickup surround so even if I did take it out, this old surround may not like it and thus open up. It's probably been on since 1968: but all is not lost as I can measure the output from the inside of the guitar and it is revealing as it measures 7.25 ohms. It is very close to the Gibson T-bucker which started to appear from around 1965, and it has been said that the 'T' stands for Treble and was embossed on the plastic bobbins to help the installer orient the pickup in the right direction. Also at around the same time, the covers changed to chrome which is what I find on Dave's guitar. So, this is no PAF pickup as many Slade forums suggest: another clue is the output. Around 1965 – 67 (no-one knows for sure) Gibson changed their manually run pickup winding system to fully automated, this resulted in more consistent 7.3 ohms to 7.5 ohms. These pickups had an A5 alnico magnet which provides more of a chime quality with top-end highs. The wood of the guitar would absorb certain frequencies and will resonate others. The pickups will translate the frequencies that the string is vibrating which is the whole reason why guitar manufacturers use different woods and certain particular hardware which affects the tone too.

Dave Hill's guitar with a large maple body and John Birch bridge would also emphasise the treble frequencies. Of course, with the rosewood fingerboard and mahogany neck it would add just enough of the mid-range tone to give this guitar a unique voice. Listen to any Slade hit and no explanation from me will describe what you can hear: it sounds unlike any other guitar I know of and coupled with the Jaguar pickup, it is unique.

In 1968 the guitar had Gibson Bonnet reflector knobs in black with a metal toggle in the lower part and the jack socket was higher up. Then around March 1973 when the John Birch bridge was fitted the look was slightly different with silver skirted control knobs similar to those you would see on an old Carlsbro amp. By the April 1975 'Slade – Live in Winterland San Francisco' gig, the lower control knob had become smaller with a small fin at each end and one control knob is lost altogether. This gig shows a great performance of Slade and in particular Dave Hill's fast vibrato and control. By 1976, all the knobs were different. The guitar is not seen much over the years as he is using various John Birch guitars and others, then in 1991 Slade release 'Radio Wall Of Sound' and on Top of the Pops, the control plate now has an extra smaller knob fitted. I can't help feel that the inspiration for this layout originally but especially now was based upon the Rickenbacker 330-360 as the small knob on the Rickenbacker was a blender control. The controls at this point are a bit taller and have small grooves on the shafts but still have chrome reflectors. The W/B/W control scratch plate is slightly thinner than the pickup covering plate and the toggle switch is also higher up now.

Today the guitar is more like its original layout except the toggle has remained higher up. As I take the rusty screws off to see underneath, the first thing I notice is that the wires used for both pickups is the wrong type. The Humbucker has a brown cable with a blue and braided wire coming out of it: this is soldered to the lower volume control which is a 500k pot connecting to the tone control with what looks like a Fender .02 ceramic type capacitor. The neck pickup has a grey coloured plastic wire that has a red and blue wire coming out of it, (something like you'd see on an old table lamp!) again connecting to the tone control with the same capacitor.

The potentiometers are unmarked but of good quality: they could be Centralabs but the middle tag doesn't look familiar. They look as if they've been in since 1968 and the shafts don't move from side to side like some cheap ones do today. A new jack socket has been fitted and the whole area looks like it is foil backed albeit patchy. Earlier I mentioned the man that built this guitar and also the suggestion by people who knew him that his wiring was not his strong point.....I can see why! It looks like both pickups have had their wires joined together with anything that was handy as they obviously could not reach the control cavity with the original wire.

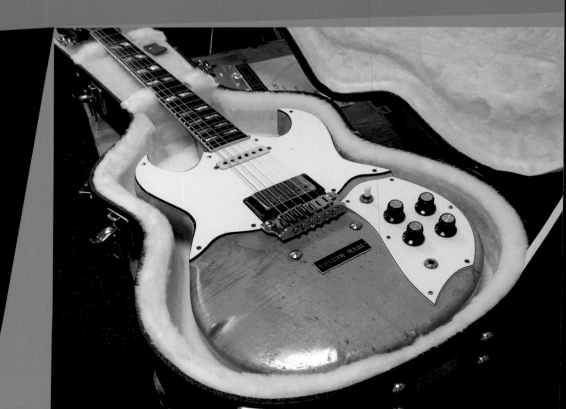

There are some well known guitars that have produced memorable riffs over the years that are embedded in the history of rock music, for me 70's rock and the classic guitar sounds that were produced before over processing crept in are hard to beat. Seeing a guitar such as this with its unique build and unique hardware in the hands of a dynamic player like Dave Hill takes some beating. This guitar has produced some of the most memorable riffs of the early 70's, enough said.

Steve Clarke meets Dave Hill

SLADE

Acknowledgements

Huge thanks to Jerry Bloom and Gary Hibbert at Wymer Publishing for their support and belief in this book.

I would like to thank the following people who have kindly helped with this book:

Matt Ingham (Cherry Red Records), Dorothy Howe, Suzi Quatro, Arthur Ramm, Bruce Welch, David Clayton (The Free Appreciation Society), Richard Henry Guitars, Peter Herwegh, (Brandin Guitars) Marian Akkerman, Jan Akkerman, The BME Liverpool, Kevin McManus, Andy Scott, Danielz (T.Rextasy), Simon Kossoff, Danny Lee, Dave Hill, the late Alan Rogan, Simon White, J.P. James, Joe D Ambrosio, Tony Visconti, Katherine Schofield (Bonhams London), John Buckton, Andy Beech, George Gruhn, Stephen Maycock (Bonhams London), Simon White, Olly Taylor, Abbie Carter, David Brewis, Clare Morris at Keith Morris Archive.

Front Cover Design by Steve Clarke.

Special Thanks to my wife Anni for her love, support and encouragement. To Gary Winterflood at Guitar Avenue for his persistence. Paul Day for his help and support. To Danny Lee for Graphics, commitment and friendship.

ABOUT THE AUTHOR

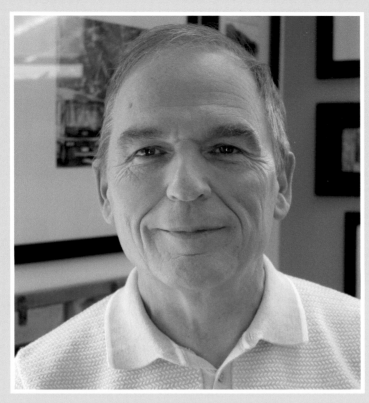

Steve has been a professional musician for over 40 years. His career began (as many do!) when he joined a band playing covers and travelling the length and breadth of the UK doing the usual social club circuits. As an accomplished lead guitarist he joined Taxi in 1978 and the band toured Europe doing gigs in their own right and as support to bands such as Smokie. Taxi had four albums released on EMI Electrola and had a fan club with 55,000 members. When Taxi split he joined a Manchester based punk band The Drones.

The Drones recorded and toured mostly in the UK. It was in this band that Steve honed his skills for song writing and with the bands singer Mike (Drone) Howells he wrote and recorded many tracks, some of which can be found on the album 'Tapes from the Attic'. It was whilst in the Drones and working closely with the bands producer Steve James (son of Carry on Syd) that Steve developed an interest in production. In 1984 Steve joined a band based in London called The Park and for three years gigged in the UK and Europe and also wrote and recorded more tracks at London's Yard studios.

As so often is the story, tired of travelling up and down the UK in vans he started to concentrate on writing and recording with his close friend, the late Paul Roberts of Drone Studio, Manchester (no connection to the band!) and together they wrote some of the music Steve is most proud of. Recording at Drone studio together, usually after a paid jingle session had finished Steve and Paul would invite other local musicians to stay behind and play on their album.

In other random events Steve played guitars on the original 12" version of the Time Warp by Damian. Steve also sang and played 20th Century Boy with Billy Idol one afternoon in a warehouse in London and coincidentally, some years later played guitar on a remix of 20th Century Boy for Mickey Finn's T.Rex.

He engineered for The Smiths on a session when they recorded 'The Boy with a Thorn in his Side'. He was guitar tech for Dave Stewart of the Eurythmics at the Manchester Royal Exchange Theatre for the premier of Ghost. He was a contributor to the Channel 4 documentary Dandy in the Underworld and the BBC's Marc Bolan: The Final Word.

Throughout all of this time (and even more so in later years) Steve has been a guitar tech with a secret penchant for physics so when it comes to understanding how low an action can go, or why certain guitar set ups respond differently due to different gauge strings Steve's your man. As well as reviewing guitars for Guitar and Bass magazine, Steve has done repairs for a vast array of customers including The Buzzcocks, Peter Hook, The Hollies, Belle and Sebastian, and one off crisis repairs for The Jason Isbell band, Chip Taylor (Wild Thing/Angel of the Morning), Teenage Fan Club, The Pixies.

Steve is still based in Manchester, UK where he lives with his wife Anni.